THE NEW
Wild Flowers
AND HOW TO GROW THEM

THE NEW
Wild Flowers
AND HOW TO GROW THEM

Enlarged and Revised Edition

by

EDWIN F. STEFFEK

Sponsored by the New England Wild Flower Society
Framingham, MA

TIMBER PRESS
Portland, Oregon
1983

PRINTED IN THE UNITED STATES OF AMERICA

TIMBER PRESS
P.O. Box 1631
Beaverton, Oregon 97075

Library of Congress Cataloging in Publication Data

Steffek, Edwin Francis, 1912–
    The new wild flowers and how to grow them.

    Rev. ed. of: Wild flowers and how to grow them.
c1954.
    Includes index.
    1. Wild flower gardening.   2. Wild flowers—North
America.   I. Title.
SB439.S8   1983   635.9'676   83-485
ISBN 0-917304-51-9

Table of Contents

PART II

Wild Flowers: Where to Find Them, and How to Transplant and Grow Them

Color Plates—65–88

THE AUTHOR'S PLEA

In more technical books this is normally the foreword, where the author makes his apologies for having written the book. Therefore, I feel it my duty to do the same.

When the first white man set foot upon this continent, it was unexploited territory, a land of abundance where plants of all kinds flourished, whether they were denizens of the woods, dwelt upon the mountain tops, or turned the western plains into seas of color.

Now, much of our forest land has been "cleared," and most of what remains has been cut over not once but several times. Our plains have been turned by the plow, and great cities now stand where once the soil was carpeted with wild flowers. New roads are continually being built and dams constructed. Even our mountain tops are no longer inviolate—radio and television stations seek to invade the heights for greater carrying range.

We cannot halt the advance of our so-called civilization, but we can at least do something to stop the wholesale disappearance of our beautiful and often already rare native plants, thus saving some of them for future generations to enjoy. Therefore, it was with this in mind that this book was written: it is an attempt to point the way, to show *what* can be done and *how*. The rest is up to you, the readers—to decide whether future generations will ever know the beauty of our native plants or not.

Although the author has long been interested in wild flowers and has roamed the woods and fields since childhood, growing many plants with varying degrees of success, he makes no claim that this book is infallible. Neither does he claim that the processes and methods herein described have been invented or discovered by him. It is with a deep sense of indebtedness that the author pays his respects to all who have gone before and contributed their bits to the accumulated knowledge of wild flower lore and culture. If at any time, anyone who reads the volume has any further or better information based upon his own findings, under his own conditions, the author will welcome his comments and criticism. It is only by such means that the cause of conservation is advanced.

With very few exceptions, the names in this book are based upon the eighth edition of *Gray's Manual of Botany*, edited by Professor Merritt Lyndon Fernald of Harvard University. For plants not there included, reliance has been placed primarily upon *Hortus Third*, by L. H. Bailey and *Wild Flowers of the United States* by Harold W. Rickett.

Lastly, may I add that especial thanks are due the late Dr. Edgar T. Wherry of the Department of Botany at the University of Pennsylvania for his careful checking of the manuscript, his constructive criticisms, and his wise counsel.

Dover, MA
November, 1982

PART ONE

An Introduction to Wild Flowers

ALONG A COUNTRY ROAD

In the cultivation of wild flowers, you are entering a bold new field, one which actually implies the extension of the genius and beauty of nature itself. Of course the rewards are many. You rightly anticipate much pleasure and profit, and a wonderful outlet for your imagination and originality. But if you hope to go nature one better, you will soon learn that with your every move you must at least follow in her footsteps. Let us start, therefore, with the way that nature has cultivated wild flowers, and analyze her methods before we attempt to imitate them.

Like all living things, plants have their friends—those with which they prefer to grow. Botanists call these groupings "plant communities" and their study "ecology," which is not half so fearsome and far more interesting than it sounds. At any rate, it seems best that we at least touch briefly upon this before we pass on to other phase of our subject, for it is in just such groupings that you should plant your wild flowers, whether setting out a small personal wild flower garden or establishing a large sanctuary.

So let us imagine we are taking a walk and come upon these various groupings as we go along. Some species are in bloom and some are not. As we leave the house, we shall start down a country road. Here we may find a mixture of many types of flora, nevertheless a very typical situation, for our roads are not laid out with any ecological principles in mind. Thus they usually offer an excellent cross-section of the flora of a given region.

First we see some common weeds such as dock, plantain, and dandelion. Then we find young goldenrods coming up and milkweeds which, later in the season, will scatter their silken parachutes. Farther along, near the edge of a small woodland, we see the large, roundish leaves of the bloodroot and perhaps a few leaves of the hepatica, while past them, under the trees, appears the large mass of a colony of mandrake or Mayapple. Now, as the roadside gets a little more bushy, we may spy the "mittens" of young sassafras trees springing up, and here, too, a few highbush blueberries have crept in. Then, in a more open, cut-over place, grow wild raspberries and fireweed, which makes such a showing in season.

Just beyond, however, we come to a large open field on our left and decide to cut across it. The first flowers that meet our eyes here are the daisies, hardy immigrants from Europe, then the equally vigorous yellow and orange hawkweeds. Here and there sprout patches of various clovers, with wild carrots and chicory. Occasionally we spot a few evening primroses, *Oenothera biennis*, and tickseed or golden coreopsis.

In the fall goldenrods, of course, and the attractive blooms of hardy asters add color to the scene. Or, in late summer, in a particularly sandy or gravelly spot, the orange butterfly weed will startle us with its blaze of color.

If the summer has just started, we may find in one corner a few wild strawberries, tempting and delicious, interspersed here and there with butter-and-eggs. Cinquefoils will wind their way between the strawberries, here and there a barren strawberry or waldsteinia, and farther over the well-known black-eyed Susan.

As we approach the far side of the field, we pass a section of junipers, both the tall Virginia and the dwarf spreading kind. Here and there the steeplebush has made itself at home, and farther along the gray birches have sprung up, with a few scattered lowbush blueberries and an occasional orange-scarlet wood lily.

We climb over the old stone wall—or perhaps an old fence in some parts of the country—and strike through a small wood of second-growth white pines. Here we see the charming pink ladyslipper and the princess-pine. Pipsissewas greet us, along with the pyrolas. Shield ferns add their graceful touch in spots, while partridge and checkerberries peep out from among the fallen pine needles and leaves. (Farther south, of course, we would probably have a pitch pine belt with more oaks and occasional tangles of catbriers.)

After a while we find the land sloping gradually down to a small brook. Here the soil is heavier and more fertile. In the muddy spots the well-known skunk cabbage comes up quite early in the spring along with the false hellebore. In the mixed growth a little above wave yellow troutlilies in season, the handsome giant trillium, and dainty yellow ladyslippers.

Downstream a bit, where the land gets still more muddy, grow our friends the marsh-marigolds, sometimes in the water and sometimes out of it. As the brook widens out into a little pond, a few cat-tails and pickerelweed emerge, as well as arrowheads and a pond-lily or two.

In the grass we almost trample on the frangrant ladies' tresses and an occasional purple-fringed orchid or two. Here, too, the dragonhead makes its home, with sometimes a cardinal flower as well as wild geraniums and bottle gentians.

After this, perhaps, we decide to jump the brook and swing up toward the oak grove on the other bank. Thus we pass the spot where the Dutchman's breeches bloom each spring and the rock where the fragile anemones nestle. Then, as we climb the slope, we detour enough to inspect our most carefully-guarded treasure, our one little patch of trailing arbutus, wishing each time that it were as plentiful as the Jack-in-the-pulpits we passed farther back or the dainty spring beauty which each year carpets the ground just ahead of us.

In some places the little yellow stargrass is becoming more plentiful with the passing of each season, along with false lily-of-the-valley and bellflowers. The graceful columbine, though, is too attractive for its own good, and in spite of its heavy seeding it barely holds its own.

The few white baneberries, or dolls' eyes, in some shady spot never fail to attract attention, just like the small purple-fringed polygalas. The equally interesting wild ginger, however, is less often noticed, inconspicuous and hidden as it is down among the leaves.

Finally, swinging around to head toward home, we cross the brook once more, this time through a hemlock-beech-maple, combination where the square twigs of blue ash and the green and white stems of mountain maple never fail, during the winter season, to catch the eye. Here in the shade the little rock-polypods literally cover the rocky ledges and a few showy orchis display their wares for passing insects.

Deep in the shade we find the ghost-like Indian pipe, with attractive evergreen Christmas ferns scattered thinly about, and on a mossy ledge a few rare walking ferns. Then, following the well-worn trail, we sniff at the malodorous scent of the purple trillium, which has spared it from overpicking. We cannot say the same, however, for its companion, the charming and delicate maiden-hair-fern. Finally, after passing our favorite colony of downy yellow violets, we get back to the road again, not too far from where we started, tired in body but refreshed in spirit.

Another day, perhaps, we visit the seashore with its shifting dunes and the beach grasses struggling valiantly to hold them in place. Here the beach peas find a haven, and the hudsonia does its best to brighten up the sandy waste, with the beach plums and the bayberries the most prominent of their larger neighbors.

Or, again, we may spend a vacation in our eastern mountains. Here we will find anew many of the same plants we already know, plus a few others such as the mountain cranberry and the tiny snowberry. In the boggy spots near the top, too, we find Labrador tea and the bog rosemary, as well as dainty arethusas and perhaps the calopogon or a few pogonias and the cloudberry or bake-apple berry.

Likewise we may find the bearberry, which we once met on the New Jersey pine barrens. The bunchberry grows everywhere on the wooded slopes with its almost constant companion, the clintonia, well-known for its blue bead-like fruits.

If we should turn our footsteps to the Southern Appalachains, we will see, along with most of our old favorites, the shortia or oconee-bells, the charming galax, and the breathtaking seas of rhododendrons. Then, if we descend to the lowlands, we can route our trip so as to pass through the territory of the famous Venus flytrap and a wealth of curious pitcherplants.

Perhaps, instead, we live in the prairie or plains country or have occasion to visit there and see what still remains of that vast sea of grass, that great supply depot from whence came many of our garden flowers, both annual and perennial. Just a few of the showiest ones to look for are the various coreopsis, gayfeathers, black-eyed Susans, butterflyweeds, gaillardias, baptisias, evening primroses and heleniums. Then, with a little more looking we may find sabatias, ladies tresses and prairie and bottle gentians, penstemons, shooting stars, bluets and a host of others. Even if you are primarily a flower enthusiast, make note of such grasses as the runner-spreading buffalo grass, blue gramma with its seeds waving in flags and the big bluestem.

Let us next change the scene to the western mountains. First, the Rockies and their outlying ranges where the Oregon grape may come into bloom as early as March on south-facing sunny slopes. In any case, spring is on the way when we see the Easter daisy or townsendia, the pasque flowers and blue-eyed Marys or collinsias. Then come the yellow wallflowers, the rare calypsos, blue columbines, penstemons, monardas, a number of gentians and shooting stars. Summer brings asters, fireweeds, red gilias, thermopsis and the yellow monkeyflower which likes to have its feet in the water. If your journey takes you high enough, keep an eye out for the marsh marigold, globe flowers, Parry's primrose, alpine phlox, glacier lilies and the tiny arenarias.

You will also see many of these same gems, if you spend some time in the Cascades and others of the more western ranges. Look for the shrubby little luetkia, the striking beargrass, Tweedy's lewisia, salmonberry, Columbia lilies, avalanche lilies, *Dicentra formosa*, salal, western rhododendrons and the western anemone with its brushlike seedheads. Also, don't miss the lupines, paintbrushes, mertensias, the unusual-looking veratrums, Jeffrey's shooting star and on the way up the western trilliums, *T. ovatum* and *rivale*.

Going down the coast the high country brings many of the same plus the Sierra star tulip. *Calochortus nudus*, California rudbeckia, pine fritillary and California roses. At the same time don't overlook the foothills and lower elevations with their California poppies, tidy tips, bird's eye gilias, more lupines, blazing stars, brodiaeas and monkeyflowers.

Finally, we must not ignore the deserts. For our purposes here we have lumped the Chihuahuan, Sonoran and Mojave Deserts all under the "Great American Desert," as is done by some geographers. Here keep a weather eye out not only for the Joshua trees, organpipes and saguaros and the chollas, ferocacti, etc. but also the many other interesting natives: the yuccas, coachwhips, catclaws, palo verdes, desert willows, mesquites and the many smaller plants that break out into bloom when the spring rains are sufficient. If the season is right, we can also count upon finding the sand verbenas, butterbush, desert senna, desert marigold, to mention just a few.

Of course, all these lists are naturally much abbreviated. There just is not room enough. Also, in Part II of this book, where we discuss the individual plants and their culture we had to leave out a great many for lack of space.

To make our wild flowers happy, we need only put them with their friends in the kinds of places they like. For a detailed breakdown of how to group them, see Table I.

HOW TO GROW WILD FLOWERS

Before you start to grow wild flowers, learn as much about them as you can. It will save you many grievous errors, eliminate much needless experimenting, and result in far greater satisfaction as well as pleasure in God's great outdoors.

Buy, or borrow from the nearest library, a few good books from which you can learn to identify the plants in your region. Find out where they grow, when they bloom, what conditions they like, and whether or not they have any quirks in their make-up. Then you are ready to go forth.

Get your experience in the woods and fields. You need not go far. Start nearby. Study the fields, the meadows, the woods, the boggy spots—in fact, any place where plants are growing naturally. Then compare them with what you read.

Study your plants. Take notes on them. Notice whether you find them in light or shade and, if in both, where they grow better. If shaded, is it a full or a part-time shade—or is it seasonal? Examine the soil. Is it sandy, peaty, loam, or leaf-mold? What kind of trees grow nearby, if any? Do they indicate an acid or a neutral soil? Don't depend too much upon a superficial examination, though. Purchase an inexpensive test kit and test the soil yourself at least occasionally.

How is the moisture supply? See whether the soil is dry or moist and whether this is generally so or of a temporary nature. Find out, if you can, how far the roots go for moisture—and you can often tell along banks, the edges of road cuts, or even along wagon ruts—without seriously disturbing the plants.

Then, look at the companion plants and see which ones normally grow side by side. This will give you an immediate hint, after you have gained enough experience, as to whether or not it is worth your while to look for certain plants in a specific locality. Also, when you find plants that are new to you, you can tell much by their companions about their natural growing conditions, their likes and dislikes.

Study the type of growth of each plant. Does it have tubers, corms, or rhizomes? Does it sucker freely? Does it grow from one stem or make a dense clump? This will often furnish a clue to its reproduction.

Observe the plants' habits. When do they first appear? When do they bloom? Do they die down inactive soon after, or do they keep on growing? Knowing these things will help you handle your own plants properly.

When you feel confident of a fair grounding in our native plants, you are ready to start growing them. Begin with a few easy ones. Make your surroundings as nearly like those in the wild as possible—within reasonable limits. Try the various methods of propagation. When you have worked up some proficiency, you can safely get into full swing. Right here, however, I might add a word of caution. Don't be over-ambitious. It is much better to care well for a few plants than to give a great many only half the care they need—and lose them.

CONSERVATION

If you really persist until you achieve some success with wild flowers, you will have the satisfaction of knowing that, beyond your personal triumph, you have made a contribution to conservation. For many years the word *conservation* had a negative implication. It meant not picking our native plants. It meant not revealing the location of rare wild flowers. It meant telling others what not to do, but it did not tell any what *to* do. Often while one group was carefully guarding the secret of some stand of rare plants, someone else with no such scruples discovered it. All of which got us nowhere.

Then came the attempt to prohibit by law the picking of certain plants. But many states passed no such laws or failed to cooperate in drawing up a uniform set of statutes. Even if they adopted such laws, most states made little or no provision for their enforcement, and showed still less interest. On top of that, if the owner of the property merely gave his consent, it superseded the law almost everywhere anyway.

All this time, therefore, people kept on picking wild flowers. New roads destroyed many plants, and dams drowned out still more. Erosion continued. Cities spread out into the country. Farmers plowed new fields, drained marshes, and cut over woods. Lumbering operations bit deeper into our stockpile of unspoiled woodlands. "Medicinal" and other plant collectors often despoiled our woods and fields. Floods wiped out still others, and carelessness permitted that greatest enemy of all—*fire*—to ravage one area after another.

All of this means only one thing—the old negative approach to conservation cannot solve the problem by itself. What we need is aggressive conservation—a *do-something* policy, not a *do-nothing* one.

Public Approach

First of all we have the obvious public or large-scale approach to this problem. More public and private reservations can and must be set aside. Some areas in practically every state still grow attractive or uncommon wild flowers not suited to man's economic needs, which we must preserve for his asthetic benefit. However, we can only do so through adequate protection, for merely to set aside an area as an acknowledged sanctuary for rare plants only courts trouble. It is an open invitation to those who innocently or not so inocently would rob some of its treasures.

Also, we must stop the over-grazing taking place on some of our national forest lands and other reservations. Only an aroused and organized public can do this, by bringing to bear a pressure greater than that now exerted by commercial interests. Similarly our national parks, where lumber, mining, and oil companies are continually trying to gain entry, need protection.

We must do away, too, with indiscriminate dumping of tin cans, ashes, bottles, old automobile bodies, and other waste materials. All such activities must be confined to refuse dumps. Where laws do not exist prohibiting unrestricted dumping, we should pass—and enforce—them.

We should take greater interest in erosion and flood control, giving active support to appropriate measures. We must control, and in many cases check, the activities of collectors of so-called "medicinal" and other plants, even though it may force them to alter their methods and occasionally to seek other employment, for the fact remains that the harm they do is irreparable. Likewise we should take action—through boycott, if necessary—to discourage the use of rare plants as decorations for Christmas or other occasions, substituting more plentiful ones.

Another thing we can do is to help establish more and better nature trails, where plants rescued from construction jobs can be set out to supplement those already present. Then the plants should not only be labeled to teach people their names, but their interesting features described, and their preservation stressed at every occasion. Here, too, lies an excellent opportunity to demonstrate the difference between "do-nothing" conservation and an active, aggressive program—how to grow more plants from seeds or by other methods without harming the originals.

These projects, suited for united or group action, deal with problems all garden clubs, women's clubs, and men's civic organizations can and should tackle. Such action will lead to a better America and reap benefits for generations to come. Resolutions alone are of no help. The important thing is *action*.

Individual Conservation

This brings us to what can be done by the individual, acting as an individual. One of the first things you can do is to learn which wild flowers may be picked with safety and which may not. In bringing up this highly controversial subject, I am perhaps leaving myself wide open for criticism from some groups. However, it still seems advisable to touch lightly upon the subject and lay down a few general rules—bearing in mind that local and state laws as well as special conditions may often invalidate them in certain localities.

First of all, preservation does not mean that no wild flowers may be picked. It does mean that none which are scarce should be picked and that even common ones should not be picked in a way that jeopardizes natural reproduction or existence. Remember at all times that even though a plant may be relatively plentiful in your own area, it may still be very scarce or rare from a countrywide viewpoint.

Remember, too, not to discourage a child from picking wild flowers. You may destroy a growing interest in one who some day may make a great contribution to the cause of preservation. Instead, guide him or her to those species which may be picked safely and explain why others must be protected. For instance, you can hardly pick a trillium without taking the leaves. Yet the leaves must be present to manufacture food for the plant to live over winter and flower next year. Likewise, when you pick a flower, it cannot set seed to produce other plants. This is especially important in the case of annuals or biennials like the fringed gentian.

To check the wisdom of picking particular flowers, see Table II.

Aside from learning how to pick flowers discriminately, you can watch for road construction and other jobs which upset plant life. Then, with permission from the parties concerned, you can arrange to remove as many as possible of the valuable or rare plants to sanctuaries, preserves, or even home grounds—if the proper conditions are being maintained there.

Next, learn how to propagate our native plants. Merely moving plants from certain destruction to a safer place will not make more of them. In fact, it will not even maintain them, because there is always some percentage of loss, however small. Therefore we must know how to grow them from seeds, root or stem cuttings, bulbs and tubers, division of the crown, offsets or layering. Here, incidentally, also lies the greatest satisfaction, in discovering and applying the secrets of nature.

After that you can re-establish plants in their former haunts with the surplus produced by the above methods. You can scatter certain seeds in likely places to excellent advantage. However, both of these methods can also lead to abuses, and we must keep a close guard at all times. All such reestablishment should be done with the knowledge and consent of the owner of the property. Also, introduce only such plants as will live in harmony with the others and are not so aggressive as to harm or drive out weaker neighbors.

Likewise, if you should happen to own any woodland, fence it in for protection against the depredations of cattle. Not only will the cattle destroy most of the smaller, more tender wild flowers but they will also pack the soil too tightly for them and chew off the next generation of trees, so necessary for the maintenance of wooded areas.

Another and very grave factor in individual conservation is the prevention of fire. Everyone can take part in this by taking every possible precaution in his personal activities, doing everything possible to counteract the danger from others' carelessness, and offering his services, if possible, when a fire does break out. Property owners can also halt the spread of forest, brush, or grass fires by constructing and maintaining proper fire lanes.

For these achievements, plus the teaching of conservation in all its phases, especially to children, every one of us must share responsibility. Those who do not offer their wholehearted cooperation, both as individuals and as members of groups, toward the goal of conservation are shirking their duty. Once the plants are gone—and it is held probable that the next fifty yeas will tell the story—it will be too late. Therefore I offer this modest volume as a part of my contribution not only to the preservation but also the restoration of our fast-disappearing wild flowers to something a little more nearly approaching their former abundance. *Your help is needed, too.*

HOW THEY GROW
Light

If we have digressed from a discussion of *how* to cultivate wild flowers, it has only been for a clarification of the *whys*. Now, coming back to the actual problems you will face, let us consider more carefully the subject of light, for this is very important. Some plants, such as the butterfly-weed, like open sunny places and gradually dwindle away in the shade. Others, such as bunchberry and clintonia, prefer a fairly heavy shade much of the day.

First, notice whether the particular species is growing in sun or shade. As pointed out earlier, you must determine whether this is a permanent situation or one which changes with the season. Bloodroots and trilliums, for instance, are often found in the sun when in bloom, but only because the leaves have not yet come out on the trees. Later, when only the foliage shows, they will enjoy the shade cast by the leaves of hardwood trees.

Next, does the situation change with the hour of the day? Many plants prefer part-time shade, delighting in a little sun during the morning or late afternoon. Others seem to tolerate considerable shade, if they get the full effect of the sun straight down at midday, or strong sunlight, given full shade part of the day.

Now, is it a light or heavy shade? If a partial shade, how heavy? Although most plants seem to prefer a dappling shade which moves with the changing position of the sun, a few, like the Indian pipe, tolerate comparative darkness.

Another factor, closely allied with shade, is the location. Some plants like a warm sunny slope. Others, such as clintonia, prefer a cool northern slope, while some which thrive in a fairly deep shade on a southern slope also do well in a more open spot on a northern one. Moreover, this changes with lattitude. Many plants, like the bunchberry, which in the more southern part of their range seek out shade and cool northern slopes or little valleys, thrive even in the full sun as they approach their northern limits.

Altitude, too, enters the picture. Very often plants which cling to the shaded spots in the warm lowlands will dwell in comparatively exposed locations on the cool mountain tops. All of which means you must study your plants' true preferences as far as possible, not just the superficial ones.

See what kind of trees, if any, grow nearby. Are they deciduous or evergreen? Evergreens, of course, give year-round shade, while the others do not. Remember, too, a fact perhaps a little off the immediate subject but hand in hand with it—some trees, like maples and elms, are notoriously shallow-rooted, while most oaks are much deeper-rooted.

In the wild garden you may determine the degree of shade in several ways. First there is the natural way with trees and shrubs, either existing or planted for the purpose. Then there is the shade cast by the buildings. Naturally the north side of a house is cooler and shadier than the south—while the eastern and western exposures are more nearly alike. If these do not meet with your particular needs, you can erect lath shades, which can be removed during cloudy weather or cooler seasons, or brush screens laid upon or woven into a more or less immovable overhead framework.

Soil

After light we must consider soil, one of the most important factors to understand, for it is not readily changed once you set out your plants. Some plants, such as the birdfoot violet and lupine, like a light, sandy or gravelly soil, while others—for example, the marsh marigold—like a heavy, mucky one. Trilliums, on the other hand, require a light, humusy soil for best results.

So look over the soil characteristics for each individual species and do your best to duplicate them before trying to grow the plant either at home or elsewhere.

With sandy or stony soil, get an idea of how coarse or how fine it is. Does it have much vegatable matter over or in it? Does it sink to any real depth, or is it only to a shallow, superficial layer? Is it a salty seashore sand (such as few plants can tolerate), or is it salt-free?

With a peaty soil you will have an altogether different set of conditions, but a few will still hold. Examine the depth of the deposit. You may find it underlaid with a substratum of different soil which really contains the roots. Of what is the peat composed—sphagnum, sedges, or other elements? Do the roots actually go down into it, or are the plants merely sitting on little "islands" in the area? Do they grow in extensive bogs or just small marshy spots?

Leafmold or humusy soils, on the other hand, also present a few new problems. Are they composed of evergreen "duff" or the leaves of deciduous trees? Since these soils nearly always occur in the woods, check the competition from tree roots. Does it contain considerable undecayed matter or has most of it reached the friable state? Loamy soils, of course, often characterize the open fields and have their own characteristic flora. However, do not be fooled. Some seemingly open areas are not true prairie soils but really woodland soils cleared in one way or another.

Once you know the texture and make-up, your next big problem is soil acidity, truly a vital one. Even with all other factors more or less suitable, if you get the degree of soil acidity wrong, the plants will usually waste away and die. This is especially true with such lime-haters as the painted trillium, *T. undulatum,* and the bunchberry, *Cornus canadensis.*

The rocks in a region sometimes indicate the soil reaction. Granite, sandstone, mica schist, and slate, in the process of weathering, generally break down to a more or less acid soil. On the other hand, marble, limestone and serpentine usually make it neutral or alkaline.

However, you cannot depend safely upon such a superficial examination alone. An actual soil test is the only sure way to determine its true nature. Often a lime-lover will apparently grow in an acid soil, but actually its roots reach down into a calcareous layer. Likewise, you will frequently find acid-soil plants growing upon a lime-bearing rock, but a closer examination will reveal that the roots are confined to an acid-soil layer above the solid substratum.

Nowadays we usually express the degree of acidity in terms of numbers based on a scale of 14. The rating of 1 represents the absolute extreme of acidity, and no plant could survive in such a soil, if it existed, while 14 is the other (alkaline) extreme—also fatal to life. Actually as far as ordinary plant life is concerned, a range of 4 to 9 is normal, with 7 known as neutral. These numbers are called pH values ("potential hydrogen ion concentration").

See Table III for details on types of soil and how to use them.

Closely bound up with the subject of soil comes the question of moisture. Often a soil which appears, at first glance, on the dry side may have an underground source of moisture. I remember a field on the brow of a hill that by all logic should be well-drained but turned out unfit for cultivation because of the very high water table. It had a layer of impervious bedrock only a foot or so beneath the surface, and all drainage water, therefore, flowed through the few inches of soil.

On the other hand, do not jump to the conclusion that a plant which inhabits bogs likes to keep its feet wet all the time. This does not necessarily follow. Even a brief inspection will show that many of the plants are actually sitting on the tops of hummocks, as often happens with orchids. Make a careful inspection, therefore, of the area in which a plant is growing before forming any final judgments.

Remember that most woods soils are damper, because of their higher humus content, than the soil of open fields. The humus, of course, retains a larger part of the water in the soil, releasing it slowly to the plants.

The shade likewise helps make woods soils generally moister and cooler than open-ground soils. The less chance the sun has to penetrate, the less the evaporation and the longer the moisture lasts. In fact, some plants in certain regions are woods dwellers in large part for the more even supply of moisture.

Still another factor we must cope with is mulch. Nearly all forest soils and, to a lesser extent, open-field soils, have a covering of slowly decaying vegetable matter over them. This not only acts as a sponge absorbing moisture and slowly letting go of it, but it also protects the soil beneath it from drying, at the same time keeping it cool for maximum root growth. Some plants, among them our native high bush blueberries, cease to grow when the soil temperature rises above 90°.

Often the soil in which we hope to grow wild flowers does not have the proper texture—a fault, unfortunately, of most home garden soils. Thus we must modify it to suit the plants. In most cases the soil suffers from a sad lack of humus. To offset this deficiency, spade in thoroughly several inches of leafmold, neutral from maples and elms or acid from oaks. Commercial peatmoss will serve, but note whether it is acid or otherwise. Of course pine duff, decomposed sawdust, or laurel and rhododendron litter will furnish desirable acidity when needed.

You will frequently find it also advisable to work into the soil a liberal quantity of coarse sand or fine gravel to improve the drainage and further discourage packing. With poor drainage it is often essential to place a six-inch or even thicker layer of sand, gravel, or cinders beneath the prepared soil. This also helps when growing rhododendrons or other acid-loving plants in limestone regions, because it tends to discourage earthworms from mixing the prepared soil with that below.

On the other hand, if the soil is already sandy or gravelly and intended to grow other than sand-loving plants, you must work plenty of humus into it as described above. If still too light, work in a little clay, silty swamp muck, or other heavy soil. Under no condition, however, should you use manures. They are too strong for most wildlings and produce an unnatural and unhealthy growth.

If you wish to grow bog or marsh plants, you must take an entirely different approach. Where a marshy area already exists, pull or grub out undesirable plants with as little disturbance to the area as possible. Otherwise the soil may turn into a sticky mud in which it will be difficult to make anything grow.

On the other hand, if you must create a new habitat, remove the soil to a depth of at least eighteen inches and line it with a clay or otherwise impervious lining. Then put in a layer of peatmoss, with perhaps a little leafmold or humus added, ten inches to a foot thick. Saturate this layer with water and stand three-inch drain tiles in it at about every four or five feet. Finally, fill the remaining space with a mixture of one-half to one-third peatmoss and the rest a good rich humusy silty soil in the case of a marsh, or mostly peat and sphagnum for a bog. The tops of the tiles should be left sticking out above the surface. By filling them with water about once a week, you can keep the area sufficiently moist for most such plants during the dry season.

Of course, in making an area of this type, you should have in mind the kind of habitate you want, for the nature of each place, as well as the plants, is different. In a bog there is little or no drainage, with the "soil" almost entirely composed of vegetable debris. Marshes, on the other hand, usually have some drainage—

often they drain into a bog—and the soil tends to be more silty.

So there are many factors to consider in the soil picture, and the wise wild flower gardener studies carefully the conditions under which the desired plants grow in nature, imitating them as closely as he can. Like genius, wild flower growing is "ten per cent inspiration and ninety per cent perspiration."

Time

To move plants successfully, keep in mind always the correct time for the undertaking. Generally speaking, they are moved best when dormant or inactive. With early spring-blooming plants this usually applies after they have finished flowering, for then the tops die down or become less active, but you can still find the plants readily.

Among those that often die down completely and disappear by midsummer are the spring-beauty, Dutchman's breeches, squirrel-corn, bloodroot, Jack-in-the-pulpit, and mertensia. These either have bulbs or thick, fleshy roots, and you may move them any time after the leaves have begun to yellow—too long a wait permits the leaves to disappear and makes it difficult to find the exact location unless marked in some way.

These plants in general are found in deciduous woods. There they bloom, store up food for next year, and then die down before the leaves above become dense and shut off most of the light, leaving one or more buds carefully hidden beneath the surface for the next year's growth.

Next come the not-quite-so-early species which, instead of dying down completely, often retain their leaves most of the season but likewise produce buds early for the next year. Among these are the ladyslippers, which are moved best somewhat later, preferably in the fall.

Still another group, including the starflowers and clintonias, renew themselves each year by means of creeping rootstocks with a bud formed at the end for the following year. To remove them, many people dig around the plants carefully, leaving the growing tip of the rootstock in the soil untouched and then wonder why their plants do not come up the following spring. With these, too, fall moving is best.

Many irises, of course, produce rhizomes and, like the garden ones, are best moved soon after flowering is over by means of a simple division. This also applies to several non-rhizomatous perennials, such as the monarda, which may be handled much like the average garden perennial.

The lilies, such as *L. canadense*, *L. philadelphicum* and *L. superbum* etc., primarily late spring or summer-blooming, do best when planted in the fall so that they can be well-established by spring. However, if the soil is not ready, you can set them out in the spring.

Of course the fall-bloomers, such as the wild asters, we generally set out in the spring. Fall moving does not give the roots time enough to become sufficiently established before cold weather sets in and the ground freezes.

To sum it up, plants that bloom early in spring are generally moved best in the fall, and those that bloom late in the season generally respond most fully when transplanted early in the spring.

Of course there are exceptions. Many plants which grow in masses and spread, like partridge-berries or common rock polypody ferns, can often be moved by peeling or cutting off a large sod and leaving them intact. You can do this almost any time of the year.

Moving Plants

Frequently it is impossible to carry out the moving during the ideal period. In such cases you can only make the best of the situation and handle the plants in whatever way they seem most likely to survive, taking hold in their new location. If possible, moisten the soil around the plants the day before. Then dig them with as much soil as practicable, and cut the tops back to within six inches or so of the ground in the case of tall plants like Joe-Pye-weed, asters, or perennial rudbeckias. Some plants, like trilliums, have only the one set of leaves and you can decrease evaporation only by removing one or more of the leaf parts or clipping off a portion of each.

After that, roll the plants carefully in moist paper and then wrap in waxed paper to retain the moisture. If the plants must be shipped or carried long distances, wash the soil carefully from the roots and wrap the latter in damp moss before placing them in the paper. However, this method is not for the amateur, since most plants transplant best with as little disturbance of the roots as possible. After transplanting, water well and shade for a few days, continuing the watering until the plants are well established.

It goes without saying that you should set out the plants at the same depth they were growing before and, as already mentioned, under the same growing conditions. For instance, orchids like the pink ladyslipper should be set so that the tip of the bud is not over an inch or so beneath the surface. To plant them too deeply only results in decay.

Also, they should be planted as they occur in nature. *Trillium grandiflorum*, for instance, a gregarious species, usually thrives in comparatively large colonies. *Trillium erectum, T. ovatum* and *T. undulatum* on the other hand, almost always grow either singly or in small groups, as do also the cardinal flower and the liatrises. To plant these too thickly detracts from the beauty of the individual blooms. But phlox, asters, and sunflowers do best in large groups. The mandrake, too, loves company. Another point to remember is that plants which die down completely in summer are better mixed with ferns or other plants if you do not want the ground bare later in the season.

With most plants place a light mulch of leaves, peatmoss or pine needles, according to their preferences, over the soil, especially the first fall, to prevent heaving. If available, a few evergreen boughs placed over this covering will further serve to insulate the plants against the vagaries of the weather and make injury from heaving less likely. True alpines and other mountain plants, such as *Potentilla tridentata*, like a mulch of stone chips, especially in summer, to keep the roots cool and retain moisture.

PROPAGATION

The next phase of wild flower culture—and perhaps the most important from the standpoing of conservation—is propagation, the creation of more plants. Without a mastery of this subject we can make no progress. It is obvious that since plants cannot live forever, new ones must take their places. So propagation is a subject we must consider very seriously. For our purposes we will divide propagation into the following five categories: seeds; division of the crowns; offsets, stolons, and layers; cuttings; bulbs, corms, rhizomes, and tubers.

Seeds

This is the best-known and usually the fastest method where you want large numbers. Generally speaking, it closely resembles the propagation of the more finicky garden perennials. The first thing you need is good fresh seed. You may purchase some from one of the few dealers in such seeds or collect it in the wild. If you do the latter, you must not only carefully record the territory at blooming time, but mark the plants themselves with stakes or tags because may species become less conspicuous after flowering season or are hidden by others.

Then keep a very close watch to get the seeds when they are ready and before they are lost. Violet seeds are forcibly propelled from the seed containers for a distance of several feet. Trailing arbutus fruits disappear, apparently with the "help" of ants, slugs, and chipmunks. Seeds of the orange butterflyweed and graceful fireweed float away on silken parachutes, while those of the gentians are shaken from their capsules by the wind. In any case, leave plenty of seed for nature to continue the race.

Next comes planting, for while most wild flower seeds may be held over for spring planting in a cool, dry place—45° to 65° is best—they usually grow better if planted at once. Old seed sometimes takes as much as two to three times as long. For best results plant them in a frame covered with screens to keep out mice, squirrels, and birds. For the soil use a mixture of equal parts of leafmold or finely-shredded peatmoss, garden loam, and sand. Acid lovers may have two parts of pine duff or oak leafmold to one each of the others.

Sowing in beds, even in frames, involves risk with many species whose seeds are small and easily buried too deeply. The small plants, likewise, are difficult to handle. Furthermore, they do not all germinate at once and the rate of growth of the seedlings varies radically—some seeds do not even produce plants until the second spring unless stored in a refrigerator for 6 to 8 weeks or more at 40°F before planting.

Therefore, planting in some sort of containers is much to be preferred. Sow the larger seeds in flats—in rows for easy transplanting—and the smaller ones scattered in pots. However, because of the danger of frost damage to the pots, large tin cans swerve the purpose better, with a row of holes punched in their sides just above the bottom and an inch or two of drainage material placed in the bottom. After sowing, moisten the soil gently but sufficiently and cover the containers to prevent too-rapid drying out. If the frame is equipped with a glass sash, you can often dispense with individual pieces of glass.

Another highly satisfactory method, particularly with very fine seed, is to place a half-inch layer of fine shredded dried sphagnum moss over the soil, sow the seeds on it, and then cover very lightly with the same material. When moistened, it retains the moisture a long time and is sterile. Transplanting is easy and the tiny rootlets have no difficulty in reaching down to the soil. Vermiculite or exploded mica works much the same way.

In any case, do not trust your memory. It can play surprising tricks. Mark each container carefully with a label bearing the name and the date of planting and also make a record of it elsewhere for future reference. Dipping the labels into clear shellac or varnish after writing will preserve the names many times longer.

Regardless of the medium, do your watering very carefully to avoid disturbing the seed. A very fine mist from an adjustable nozzle or a compressed air sprayer is often best. Standing containers in water until the soil is moist is safer.

With most species the seedlings may be pricked off and replanted into small flats. Plant bands, fertilizer-impregnated or not, in the flats make subsequent handling even easier. In all cases it requires great care, with the flats watered at once and protected from the sun for a few days with sheets of newspaper.

Shade, too, does a great deal to prevent overheating of the frames and drying out. However, placing the frames under the shade of trees usually proves unsatisfactory because you cannot regulate the degree of light and you often get competition from the tree roots. Far superior is a screen made of laths placed one lath-width apart, which can be taken off entirely on cloudy days. If possible, run the slats north and south. Brush on an overhead frame is also good, although you cannot remove it easily for short periods.

Sowing as soon as ripe, as advocated earlier, has several advantages. A few very early-blooming plants will produce seedlings the same year. It does not expose the seeds to the danger of drying out before planting, and it favors those seeds which need a period of "after-ripening," embryo-development within the seed at low temperature.

For the first winter, especially, mulch the plantings in the frames. This will prevent a too-rapid drying out of the soil and heaving, especially dangerous to young plants, as it tears them from their roots. Use straw, evergreen boughs, salt marsh hay, or cranberry tops. Glass wool has been tried and found excellent but expensive.

After the seedlings have attained sufficient size in the flats you may carry them along further in pots plunged to the rims in well-drained frames, planted in especially prepared soil in the frames or, in some cases, directly into their permanent locations. Ordinarily this takes place the second spring, although with some slow-growing plants it may take a year longer. Blooming usually commences the second or third year.

Division

As with most garden perennials and rock plants, division of the crowns may often be practiced. This does not produce as many plants in a short time, but, if fewer, they are generally stronger at first and come into bloom sooner. Next to sowing seed, this is probably the most widely-used method of propagation.

In general most of the wild flowers fall into three different groups. Some increase by throwing out creeping rootstocks or by stems above the ground. We will discuss this further along with layering. Others increase the number of buds arising from the roots—as happens with most cypripediums. Still others, like tall phloxes and fall asters, simply increase the size of clumps.

The best time to make the division is when the plants are not in active growth—early spring or late summer and early fall. In general, those plants which bloom early in the season, such as *Phlox divaricata* and bloodroot, are best divided later in the year, those which bloom in summer or fall, such as the closed or bottle gentian, are best divided in early spring just as growth is commencing. In this way the plants undergo the least shock.

The actual division itself is simple. Dig the plants up and shake them free of soil. If they are very small, you can wash them. This makes it possible to see the natural divisions of the plant. Then gently pull or cut them apart with a sharp knife. Cut portions of large roots, such as those of the bloodroot, may be dusted with sulphur to discourage decay from setting in.

The number of divisions made from one clump will vary with the individual and his desires. You may make strong clumps of several shoots each or divide the plant into as many pieces as there are shoots or natural subdivisions. Naturally, the more you make and the smaller they are, the weaker will be the resulting plants and the longer the time needed to make large plants. But it does give you greater abundance.

After making these divisions, you may set the new plants out in frames or nursery beds to become established or plant them directly into their permanent locations. The former method is preferable with all except the strongest growers.

In any case, the new plants should be mulched for the first winter with marsh hay, straw, or evergreen boughs as described above. This will prevent heaving out of the soil with its consequent tearing of the roots during periods of freezing and thawing.

Stem and Root Cuttings

Propagation by cuttings falls into three major groups—green or softwood cuttings, dormant or hardwood cuttings, and root cuttings. All are valuable with plants which grow slowly from seeds or possess certain variations which are desirable to perpetuate—variations which usually do not come true from seed except in a small percentage of cases. As two examples, we can cite particularly deep pink plants of trailing arbutus or yellowish butterfly-weeds.

Of these three methods, the first is perhaps the most commonly practiced with wild flowers. It works with both herbaceous and many woody materials. In the case of herbaceous plants, take the cuttings, preferably, early in the season, before the hot dry weather comes. Cut the stems of the plants into sections with leaves, usually four to six inches long, making the lower cut generally just below a node, joint, or leaf, and removing the top or not according to the length and degree of maturity of the stem. Soft, sappy growth is of little value.

Then you remove the lower leaves and place the cuttings upright in sand, sand and peat, or vermiculite, with one-third to one-half buried in the sand. The second medium of sand and peat is used primarily for such members of the heath family as the trailing arbutus and rhodora. Vermiculite has proved particularly successful with many species of plants.

Where the quantities justify it, the rooting medium is best placed in a frame or hotbed and given a gentle bottom heat, either from a six-inch layer of packed horse manure or, much better, from an electric heating cable equipped with an adjustable thermostat. Over the top place an ordinary glass sash to retain a humid atmosphere and prevent drying. However, to keep the air temperature within the frame from running too high the glass is better painted with a coat of white lead and gasoline. Over this you may place lath screens such as described earlier, removable on cloudy days.

After "planting" the cuttings, keep the sand or other material moist by watering lightly one or more times a day, as necessary. For faster rooting, try one of the prepared commercial rooting compounds. However, these require care to use the correct strength.

Small numbers may be rooted in a flower pot covered with a mason, bell or tobacco jar. Otherwise, the method remains the same. You may do the watering by standing the pot in a pan of water and allowing it to soak up the water until the surface is moist. Another way is to plunge a small pot in the center, after having first plugged its drainage hole with a cork. Then, if you fill this empty inner pot with water, it slowly seeps through and keeps the surrounding material moist.

Still another, and newer, method is to wrap polyethylene film over a frame, covering the flat or pot completely. This way one watering may last for months.

Hardwood cuttings are taken only of woody plants such as the various shrubs. The cuttings are taken in the fall after the wood has been matured and are generally stored in bundles in a cold, but not freezing cellar or storage house. They are usually placed either horizontally or upside down in slightly moist sand, peat, or other material. Then in late winter or early spring the cuttings which have calloused over may be taken out and placed in one of the rooting mediums listed above in a greenhouse bench with gentle bottom heat. After that the treatment is essentially the same.

Some of the more easily-rooted species such as the wild grapes or bittersweet may be held in the cold storage until very early spring. Then you may set them out right side up, one-third to one-half their depth, in rows in the open soil. In either case you may use one of the rooting compounds, dipping the cuttings in it before you put them away to callous over.

Root cuttings are generally taken of plants with thick roots such as the butterfly-weed, pieces of root of which left in the ground have sometimes grown new tops and thus started new plants by themselves. However, to speed up the process, root cuttings may be taken in May and will soon provide satisfactory plants.

On the other hand, many root cuttings are made in the fall or early winter, being pieces of the larger roots two or three inches long. They are first allowed to callous over, buried in moist sand in a well-mulched cold frame, and then brought indoors in March. Although some root sufficiently well in a horizontal position, others, like the butterfly-weed, do better placed vertically with the "stem-end" uppermost, barely under the surface of a light soil. However, if you cannot remember which is the top and which the bottom, place the cuttings horizontally. The plant knows which is which. When there is no greenhouse available, the cuttings can often be rooted in hotbeds or cold frames later in the spring. In the case of the Solomon's seals they may lie dormant all the next season.

Others which may be started from root cuttings are the fringed polygala and the bloodroot. Fringed polygala cuttings do best in an acid leafmold. The shinleaf does fairly well in an acid peat.

Bulbs, Corms, Rhizomes, Stolons, and Tubers

Here we have several means of propagation all very much alike. It might be well, here, to start with a few definitions. A bulb is an enormously thickened leafbud placed underground for the storage of food. It may have closely-fitting scales like the alliums or narrower, looser scales like the lilies. A corm, on the other hand, is solid throughout, being actually a bulblike thickened stem covered with a thin "tunic" or covering like the gladiolus.

Bulbs frequently separate into two or more nearly equal parts, permitting easy division into two separate plants. However, a far more rapid method of propagation is to remove from the parent bulbs the numerous bulblets which form around some of them. Then plant these in a fairly light soil, covered lightly, and you may look for blooming-sized plants in from one to three years.

Still another way is to remove some of the thick outer scales from the bulb and plant them in the same manner. Half sand and half leafmold works very well in most cases. This generally applies to such plants as the lilies and may be done after flowering or even in late fall or early winter. Since they usually take at least two years to produce plants of any size, you can best handle the scales in pots or flats.

Next come rhizomes, often thickened partly underground root-stems, generally with leafy shoots from their upper surface and roots from the lower. We find good examples in the iris clan. Propagation is readily accomplished by cutting the rhizomes into several parts according to the natural divisions, obvious even to the most inexperienced.

Closely allied with the rhizomes are the stolons, slender branches, generally above ground, rooting at the tip or at joints as in the case of certain grasses. In either case, you can easily accomplish propagation by cutting off the rooted portions, and growing them on as individual plants.

A tuber, on the other hand, is a shorter, fleshy underground stem or shoot. It may have roots at one end and stem buds at the other, as in the dahlia, or eyes producing both types of growth scattered over its entire body. In either case the individual tubers may be separated and planted individually to form separate plants, and the potato-like ones cut up still further into pieces containing one or more eyes.

A runner generally refers to a stolen—a slender prostrate branch which roots at the joints or end, like the dalibarda and foam flower.

ENEMIES

In growing wildflowers, we must of course overcome enemies other than man and his works which threaten our native plants. These we can understand and control without too much difficulty. Ordinarily, in small, rather intimate plantings—or with certain especially choice items—the control of insects and diseases may enter into the picture. In large or extensive developments such care is usually neither feasible nor, in fact, as necessary as in our gardens, because we rarely grow wild flowers in large unbroken masses. With the plants fewer in number and farther apart, they do not create the extensive food supply which gives insects and diseases free rein.

In general there are two major types of insect pests—the chewing insects which actually eat holes in the plant tissues and the sucking insects which merely insert a tube into the tissues and suck out the juices. (A third group, the rasping insects, is usually controlled in the same way as the latter group.) For the first type we use an approved stomach poison applied according to the manufacturer's directions, covering the leaves and tender stems thoroughly, and keeping them so throughout the danger period. One example of the damage these insects do is the holes chewed in violet leaves. The chief offenders in this group are the various beetles and caterpillars.

The sucking insects, of course, cannot be reached with stomach poisons. Therefore, we must resort to materials which will kill them upon contact, the best-known being nicotine sulphate, pyrethrum, rotenone and Malathion. Stomach poisons will not help us here. In fact, they kill off the natural enemies of many of these pests and thus thwart our purpose. Perhaps the best example of the sucking pest is the plant lice which almost invariably infect the native lupine species. Spray thoroughly, hitting the insects, once every week or ten days as long as any danger continues.

Red spiders—so minute they can scarcely be seen with the naked eye—may attack the larger, woody plants, sucking out the juices and giving the leaves a brownish cast. We can best stop them with a strong stream of water from a hose. This washes them off the plants, and because of their tiny size they cannot get back to any great extent in a wild garden.

Hand in hand with the two groups mentioned above we have the cutworms and slugs—"snails" without shells—and true snails. These do great damage by chewing, often attacking especially the rarer orchids when grown in the small wild flower garden and destroying them completely in a very short time. The best method of control is to scatter one of the prepared cutworm baits thinly among the plants, especially in the evening, as soon as any danger presents itself. Repeat this as necessary. The oft-recommended beer is rather erratic in its results.

Diseases rarely occur, except mildew, which appears during damp periods, especially if poor drainage of air prevails. Better spacing of the plants is the best cure. Another and more serious trouble is damping off, which attacks and kills many seedlings almost overnight. Where this appears, bake the soil or sow the seeds in some sterile medium such as clean sand, fine-chopped sphagnum, or vermiculite. Sterilizing the seeds chemically is also possible sometimes, but to date growers have done little work along this line with our wild flowers.

Indoor Culture

If you wish to experiment, you can bring many of the spring wild flowers into bloom indoors ahead of season. However, I do not advocate this unless you are certain to give them the care they require and will plant them out carefully later so as to prevent any destruction of our already long-suffering wild flowers.

In general, the earlier a plant blooms, or the nearer its blooming season you try to force it, the easier the process. The time required varies from the two or three weeks needed for the hepaticas to two months or more for the ladyslippers.

Although most of them can be lifted in late fall just before the ground freezes and stored in moist sand or soil in a cold cellar, it is better to pot them up in late summer or early fall—so long as they are dormant. In this way the plants will suffer less injury and can establish better root systems before blooming time arrives. Thus the flowering will not only be superior, but the plants will be in much better shape to set outdoors after the blooming is over.

After planting, place the pots or flats in a shed or deep coldframe, plunging the pots to their rims to discourage breaking by frost. When the soil has become frozen, cover them lightly with leaves, marsh hay, straw, or other non-packing mulch, and put on a board cover. Ventilation is necessary, however, to prevent decay.

When you want to take the pots or flats indoors, usually some time after Christmas or New Year's, you can readily loosen them with warm water. Allow at least eight weeks in storage before forcing, and longer is better.

After taking up the pots or flats, you may best leave in a cool cellar to thaw out slowly. Then gradually increase the temperature. When the plants show signs of activity, remove them to a light, airy place. Keep the temperature rather low at all times, allowing it to increase very slowly and then not over room temperature. At no time should the plants be permitted to suffer from lack of water and, if the sun's rays become too intense, a light shade may prove helpful.

The soil for such forcing should be of the type normally preferred by the plant, anyway, but lightened somewhat by the addition of some sharp sand.

Likewise, plenty of drainage material should be placed in the bottom of the container. Generally one large pot with several plants brings much better results than small pots with individual plants. This method lessens the danger of drying out, makes it much easier to maintain better growing conditions, and usually provides more room for the roots to run than when cramped into a small pot.

Among the plants amenable to such handling are the following:

The hepaticas are perhaps the easiest and quickest of all. Three plants to a six-inch pan makes a nice showing. Only two to three weeks are usually necessary under favorable growing conditions. *H. acutiloba* prefers a more or less neutral soil and *H. americana* a somewhat acid one with light shade.

The claytonias are almost as easy. Set the tiny tubers rather shallowly in a well-drained leafmoldy soil, placing them somewhat thickly, since the plants are so tiny.

Another is the charming little Dutchman's breeches. Set the little tuber-like roots about one inch deep. The same holds for its close relative, the squirrel corn.

Trailing arbutus is likewise very early. Unless it is already a pot-grown plant, the whole sod should be taken up, so as not to disturb the roots.

Another not-too-difficult one is the marsh-marigold or *Caltha palustris*. Give it a little more water than the others. It can be flowered readily in February.

The dainty little anemone or windflower, *A. quinquefolia,* is also comparatively easy, also the equally charming and longer flowering *Anemonella thalictroides.*

The shortia from our southern mountains may be a little harder and does better when well-established first. Give it an acid, humusy soil. Its glossy leaves make it one of our handsomest low plants for forcing.

Most of the trilliums behave fairly well, although *T. grandiflorum, luteum* and *nivale* are among the most amendable. The first two are noticeably larger plants and consequently should be planted much deeper, two to three inches below the surface.

Tiarella cordifolia, the foamflower, is also one of the best, with large clumps particularly desirable.

These are only a few. *Silene caroliniana pensylvanica* often forces readily. Mertensia does well, although larger and coarser than most of these. The phloxes, both *P. divaricata* and *subulata,* can be brought into bloom ahead of season. The same is true of *Helonias bullata,* Jack-in-the-pulpit, early saxifrage, wild ginger, the crested and lake irises, yellow star-grass, dodecatheon, and nearly all the violets.

You can even handle some of the orchids in this way, the yellow-lady-slipper, perhaps, the most easily. Another is *Cypripedium reginae,* the showy ladyslipper. Give them a light humusy soil. If you attempt *C. acaule* or *arietinum,* make doubly sure the soil is on the acid side, while for the small white one, *C. candidum,* add a little lime. In any case place the bud just beneath the surface and spread the roots out carefully. The showy orchids, calypso, and rattlesnake plantain have also been successfully forced.

In all indoor culture, after the flowers have passed, keep the plants in active growth, keep them cool, and plant them out of doors in suitable locations as soon as the season is sufficiently advanced. With some species dormancy will occur earlier than usual, but no harm will result. Although with the very easiest, like the hepatica, you may force them year after year, this is not advisable as a general rule.

Whether for indoor culture, as touched upon above, or for culture outdoors, which you are more likely to undertake, you will find in Part II a useful guide to individual species, their habits and needs.

TABLE I

SOME REPRESENTATIVE WILD FLOWERS: WHERE TO FIND THEM

Open Field and Juniper Communities

†*Ceanothus americanus*	New Jersey tea
†*Comptonia peregrina*	sweet fern
†*Juniperus communis depressa*	ground juniper
†*Myrica pensylvanica*	bayberry
†*Potentilla fruticosa*	shrubby cinquefoil
†*Robinia hispida*	rose-acacia
†*Rubus*, misc.	blackberries, raspberries, etc.
†*Spiraea latifolia*	meadowsweet
†*Spiraea tomentosa*	steeplebush
**Achillea millefolium*	yarrow
Anaphalis margaritacea	pearly everlasting
Asclepias syriaca	common milkweed
Asclepias tuberosa	butterfly weed
Aster, misc.	the asters
**Chrysanthemum leucanthemum*	daisy
**Cichorium intybus*	chicory
*Daucus carota	Queen Anne's lace
Dennstaedtia punctilobula	hay-scented fern
Epilobium angustifolium	fireweed
Fragaria virginiana	wild strawberry
*Hieracium, misc.	hawkweeds
Houstonia caerulea	bluets
Liatris, misc.	gayfeathers
Lilium philadelphicum	wood lily
*Linaria vulgaris	butter-and-eggs
Lobelia siphilitica	blue cardinal-flower
Lupinus perennis	lupine
Oenothera, misc.	evening primroses
**Prunella vulgaris*	self-heal
Pteridium aquilinum	bracken fern
Ranunculus, misc.	buttercups
Rudbeckia hirta	black-eyed Susan
**Saponaria officinalis*	bouncing-Bet
Saxifraga virginiensis	early saxifrage
Sisyrinchium angustifolium	blue-eyed grass
Solidago, misc.	goldenrods
*Trifolium, misc.	clovers
**Verbascum thapsus*	mullein

†Shrubby or semi-shrubby.
*Plants introduced from Europe or elsewhere.

White Pine Woods

Chimaphila umbellata cisatlantica	pipsissewa
Chimaphila maculata	striped pipsissewa
Cypripedium acaule	pink ladyslipper
Dryopteris marginalis	marginal shield fern
Gaultheria procumbens	wintergreen
Lycopodium, misc.	club-mosses
Maianthemum canadense	false lily-of-the-valley
Mitchella repens	partridgeberry
Pteridium aquilinum	bracken fern
Pyrola elliptica	shinleaf

The Brookside Plants

†*Alnus incana*	speckled alder
†*Amelanchier canadensis*	shadbush
†*Clethra alnifolia*	sweet pepperbush
†*Hamamelis virginiana*	witch-hazel
†*Ilex verticillata*	black-alder holly
†*Rhododendron viscosum*	white swamp azalea
Acorus calamus	sweetflag
Arisaema triphyllum	Jack-in-the-pulpit
Arisaema dracontium	dragon-root
Asarum canadense	wild-ginger
Caltha palustris	marsh-marigold
Chelone glabra	turtlehead
Erythronium americanum	trout-lily
Eupatorium purpureum	sweet Joe-Pye-weed
Gentiana andrewsi	closed gentian
Geranium maculatum	wild geranium
Habenaria psycodes	purple-fringed orchid
Impatiens capensis	jewel weed
Iris versicolor	blue flag iris
Lilium canadense	Canada lily
Lilium superbum	Turks' cap lily
Lobelia cardinalis	cardinal flower
Onoclea sensibilis	sensitive fern
Osmunda cinnamomea	cinnamon fern
Osmunda claytoniana	interrupted fern
Osmunda regalis	royal fern
Smilacina racemosa	false spikenard
Spiranthes, misc.	ladies' tresses
Symplocarpus foetidus	skunk cabbage
Thalictrum dioicum	early meadow-rue
Trillium erectum	purple trillium
Uvularia sessilifolia	oakesia, wild oats
Veratrum viride	false hellebore
Viola, misc.	violets

Water-lovers and Pond Dwellers

†*Cephalanthus occidentalis*	buttonbush
†*Clethra alnifolia*	sweet pepperbush
†*Rhododendron viscosum*	white swamp azalea
†*Salix*, misc.	willows
Acorus calamus	sweetflag
Caltha palustris	marsh marigold
Lobelia cardinalis	cardinal flower
*Lythrum salicaria	spiked loosestrife
Menyanthes trifoliata	bogbean
Myosotis scorpioides	forget-me-not
Nelumbo lutea	American lotus
Nuphar advena	yellow pondlily
Nymphaea odorata	pondlily
Orontium aquaticum	golden club
Peltandra virginica	arrow-arum
Polygonum punctatum	water smartweed
Pontederia cordata	pickerelweed
Sagittaria latifolia	arrowhead
Sparganium, misc.	bur-reeds
Typha latifolia	common cat-tail

Typical Bog Plants—Acid Soil

†*Andromeda glaucophylla*	bog rosemary
†*Chamaedaphne calyculata*	leatherleaf
†*Ilex verticillata*	black-alder holly
†*Kalmia angustifolia*	sheep laurel
†*Kalmia polifolia*	bog laurel
†*Ledum groenlandicum*	Labrador tea
Arethusa bulbosa	arethusa
Calopogon pulchellus	grasspink
Cornus canadensis	bunchberry
Drosera, misc.	sundews
Eriophorum, misc.	cotton grasses
Gaultheria hispidula	creeping snowberry
Habenaria, misc.	fringed orchids
Pogonia ophioglossoides	rose pogonia
Rubus chamaemorus	bake-apple berry
Sarracenia, misc.	pitcher plants
Vaccinium, misc.	cranberries and blueberries

The Oak-Hickory Woods

†*Cornus florida*	flowering dogwood
†*Hamamelis virginiana*	witch hazel
†*Kalmia latifolia*	mountain laurel
†*Rhododendron nudiflorum*	pinxterflower
†*Rubus odoratus*	purple-flowering raspberry
†*Vaccinium angustifolium*	lowbush blueberry
Actaea pachypoda and rubra	white and red baneberries
Anemone quinquefolia	wood anemone
Anemonella thalictroides	rue anemone

Aquilegia canadensis	columbine
Asarum canadense	wild ginger
Asplenium platyneuron	ebony-spleenwort
Aster, misc.	asters
Chimaphila maculata	striped pipsissewa
Claytonia virginica	spring beauty
Dryopteris marginalis	shield fern
Gaultheria procumbens	wintergreen
Hepatica americana	hepatica
Hypoxis hirsuta	yellow stargrass
Maianthemum canadense	false lily-of-the-valley
Mitchella repens	partridge-berry
Mitella diphylla	bishop's -cap
Orchis spectabilis	showy orchis
Polygala paucifolia	fringed polygala
Polystichum acrostichoides	Christmas fern
Pyrola elliptica	shinleaf
Sanguinaria canadensis	bloodroot
Tiarella cordifolia	false mitrewort

Hemlock, Maple, Beech Combination

†*Acer pensylvanicum*	moosewood
†*Amelanchier canadensis*	shadbush
†*Cornus florida*	flowering dogwood
†*Hamamelis virginiana*	witch hazel
†*Kalmia latifolia*	mountain laurel
†*Taxus canadensis*	American yew
†*Viburnum alnifolium*	hobblebush
Actaea pachypoda and rubra	baneberries
Adiantum pedatum	maidenhair fern
Asarum canadense	wild ginger
Clintonia borealis	clintonia
Cypripedium calceolus pubescens	large yellow ladyslipper
Dicentra cucullaria	Dutchman's breeches
Dryopteris hexagonoptera	broad beech-fern
Epigaea repens	trailing arbutus
Erythronium americanum	troutlily
Lycopodium, misc.	club-mosses
Maianthemum canadense	false lily-of-the-valley
Mitella diphylla	bishop's-cap
Medeola virginiana	Indian cucumberroot
Orchis rotundifolia	small round-leaved orchis
Orchis spectabilis	showy orchis
Oxalis montana	common wood sorrel
Streptopus roseus	rosy twisted-stalk
Trientalis borealis	starflower
Trillium grandiflorum	great trillium
Trillium erectum	purple trillium
Uvularia perfoliata	bellwort
Viola pubescens	downy yellow violet

Pine Barrens Plants

†*Leiophyllum buxifolium*	sandmyrtle
†*Myrica pensylvanica*	bayberry
†*Vaccinium angustifolium*	lowbush blueberry
†*Vaccinium corymbosum*	highbush blueberry
†*Comptonia peregrina*	sweetfern
Arctostaphylos uva-ursi	bearberry
Cypripedium acaule	pink ladyslipper
Epigaea repens	trailing arbutus
Gentiana autumnalis porphyrio	pine-barren gentian
Hudsonia tomentosa	beach-heath
Lupinus perennis	lupine
Pteridium aquilinum	bracken fern
Pyxidanthera barbulata	pyxie
Solidago, misc.	goldenrods
Viola pedata	birdfoot violet

The Eastern Mountains
(North)

Oxalis montana	wood sorrel
Trillium undulatum	painted trillium
Clintonia borealis	bluebeads
Coptis groenlandica	goldthread
†*Viburnum alnifolium*	hobblebush
Cornus canadensis	bunchberry
Epilobium angustifolium	fireweed
Vaccinium vitis-idaea minus	miniature mountain cranberry
Habenaria dilatata	tall, leafy wild orchid
Potentilla tridentata	three-toothed cinquefoil
Silene acaulis	moss campion
Arenaria groenlandica	mountain sandwort
Campanula rotundifolia	bluebell
Diapensia lapponica	diapensia
†*Kalmia polifolia*	pale laurel
†*Cassiope hypnoides*	moss plant
†*Phyllodoce caerulea*	mountain heath
Geum pecki	mountain avens
†*Loiseleuria procumbens*	alpine azalea
†*Rhododendron lapponicum*	Lapland rosebay
†*Empetrum nigrum*	black crowberry
†*Ledum groenlandicum*	Labrador tea
†*Arctostaphylos uva-ursi*	bearberry
Gaultheria hispidula	creeping snowberry
Linnaea borealis	twinflower

(South)

Many of the above, plus others such as the following:

Clintonia umbellulata	speckled wood lily
Convalaria montana	American lily-of-the-valley

Amianthium muscaetoxicum	fly poison
Lilium grayi	gray's lily
Hexastylis shuttleworthi	heart-leaved wild ginger
Silene virginica	fire pink
Trillium, misc.	trilliums
†*Magnolia fraseri*	mountain magnolia
†*Calycanthus floridus*	sweet shrub
Dicentra eximia	bleeding heart
Dentaria laciniata	toothwort
†*Fothergilla major*	fothergilla
†*Cladrastis lutea*	yellow wood
†*Rhododendron catawbiense*	catawaba rhododendron
†*Rhododendron maximum*	rosebay or great laurel
†*Rhododendron calendulaceum*	flame azalea
†*Leiophyllum buxifolium*	sand myrtle
Chelone lyoni	pink turtlehead
Coreopsis pubescens	coreopsis
†*Halesia carolina*	silverbell tree
Galax aphylla	galax
Geum radiatum	Appalachian avens

The Prairies and Plains

Phlox oklahomensis	Oklahoma phlox
Coreopsis lanceolata	lance-leaved coreopsis
Coreopsis tinctoria	calliopsis, annual coreopsis
Delphinium tricorne	dwarf delphinium
Baptisia leucophaea	pale false indigo
Rudbeckia hirta (R. serotina)	black-eyed Susans
Gaillardia pulchella	showy gaillardia
Helenium autumnale	helenium or sneezeweed
Liatris pychnostachya	Kansas gayfeather
Liatris squarosa	scaly blazing star
Oenothera missouriensis	Ozark sundrop
Asclepias tuberosa	butterflyweed
Hypoxis hirsuta	yellow star grass
Erythronium albidum	white troutlily
Spiranthes romanzoffiana	hooded ladies tresses
Ratibida columnaris	Mexican-hat
Cassia fasciculata	partridge pea
Monarda citriodora	lemon horse-mint
Salvia azurea	blue salvia
Gentiana andrewsi	bottle gentian
Eustoma grandiflorum	prairie gentian
Aster, misc.	asters
Solidago, misc.	goldenrods
Lilium michiganense	Michigan lily
Dodecatheon meadia	eastern shooting star

†*Mahonia repens*	creeping Oregon grape
Townsendia exscapa	mountain daisy
Erysimum capitatum	yellow wallflower
Delphinium ramosum	Colorado larkspur
Iris Missouriensis	Missouri iris
Mertensia alpina	alpine mertensia
Aquilegia caerulea	Colorado columbine
Penstemon, misc.	penstemons
Lupinus sericeus	lupine, wolfbean
Dodecatheon pulchellum	showy shooting star
Thermopsis montana	golden pea
Mimulus guttatus	yellow monkey flower
Caltha biflora	western marsh marigold
Trollius laxus	globe flowers
Primula parryi	Parry's primrose
Pyrola picta	painted shinleaf or pipsisewa
Sedum rhodanthum	rose crown
Phlox multiflora	spreading phlox
Hymenoxys (Rydbergia) grandiflora	alpine goldflower
Erysimum amoenum	"purple" wallflower
Gentiana thermalis	western fringed gentian
Swertia radiata	green gentian
Lloydia serotina	alpine lily
†*Cercocarpus montanus*	mountain mahogany
†*Rubus parviflorus*	thimbleberry

(Cascades and Neighboring Areas)

Lysichitum americanum	western skunk cabbage
Trillium ovatum, rivale, petiolatum	western trilliums
Asarum candatum	long-tailed wild ginger
Clintonia uniflora	white clintonia, queen's cup
Pyrola asarifolia	ginger shinleaf
†*Gautheria shallon*	salal
†*Vaccinium parvifolium*	red huckleberry
†*Menziesia ferruginea*	menziesia
†*Rubus spectabilis*	salmonberry
Caltha leptosepala	oval-leaved western marsh marigold
Erythronium grandiflorum, montanum	glacier and avalanche lilies
Anemone occidentale	old-man-of-the-mountains
Phlox diffusa	mountain phlox
Lilium columbianum, parvum	Columbia and alpine lilies
†*Cassiope mertensiana*	white heather
†*Phyllodoce empetriformis*	red heather
Veratum viride, californicum	green false hellebore, corn lily
Aquilegia formosa	Sitka columbine

†*Rhododendron albiflorum*	white-flowered rhododendron
Mimulus tilingi, lewisi	yellow and rosy monkey flowers
Lewisia rediviva	bitterroot
Luetkia pectinata	partridge foot
Penstemon, misc.	penstemons
Xerophyllum tenax	beargrass
Camassia quamash	camas

Central and Southern California
(The Higher Country)

†*Phyllodoce breweri*	alpine heather
Abronia alpine	mountain sand verbena
Dodecatheon alpinum, jeffreyi	alpine, Sierra shooting stars
Orthocarpus luteus	yellow owl clover
Calochortus nudus	Sierra star tulip
Fritillaria pinetorum	pine fritillary
Gilia (Ipomopsis) aggregata	scarlet gilia
Rudbeckia californica	Sierra coneflower
Penstemon palmeri	Palmer's penstemon
Ranunculus californicus	California buttercup
Aster adscendens	purple mountain aster
Aconitum columbianum	monkshood
Viola lobata	pine violet
†*Rosa californica*	California rose
†*Rhododendron occidentale*	western azalea
Dentaria californica	milkmaids

(Mostly Lower Altitudes)

Eschscholtzia californica	California poppy
Erysimum asperum	western wall flower
Dodecatheon clevelandi patulum	lowland shooting star
Mentzelia lindleyi	evening star
Calochortus luteus, venustus	yellow and white mariposa
Gilia tricolor	bird's eye's gilia
Fritillaria pluriflora, pudica	adobe lily, yellow fritillary
Mimulus tricolor, palmeri	tricolored and Palmer's monkey flowers
Oenothera dentata	evening primrose
Aster chilensis	purple aster
Viola pedunculata	yellow pansy
Layia platyglossa	tidy tips
Clarkia unguiculata (C. elegans)	showy clarkia
Brodiaea pulchella, californica	blue Dicks, and California brodiaea
Abronia umbellata	sand verbena

The Southwest

Cornegiea gigantea	saguaro
Lemaireocerems marginatus	organ pipe cactus
Ferocactus wislizeni	barrel cactus

Opuntia bigelovi, leptocaulis, fulgida	Teddy bear, Christmas and jumping chollas
†*Fauquieria splendens*	ocotillo or coachwhip
Agave, misc.	century plants
Yucca, misc.	yuccas
†*Cercidium floridum*	palo verde
†*Acacia greggi*	catclaw acacia
†*Prosopis glandulosa*	honey mesquite
†*Larrea divaricata*	creosote bush
†*Encelia farinosa*	incense or brittlebush
Abronia fragrans	fragrant sand verbena
Nama demissum	purplemat
Psilostrophe tagetina	paperflower
Eschscholzia californica	California poppy
Lupinus subcarnosus, etc.	Texas bluebonnet, etc.
Zinnia grandiflora	desert zinnia
Sidalcea neomexicana	globemallow
Machaeranthera tortifolia	Mojave aster
Delphinium parishi	Parish's delphinium
Mirabilis multiflora	many-flowered four o'clock
Argemone corymbosa	prickly poppy

Table II

WILDFLOWERS WHICH MAY BE PICKED

Flowers Which May Be Picked Freely

Asters	Jewelweed
Bindweeds	Joe-Pye-weed
Black-eyed Susans	Meadow-rue
Bluets	Milkweeds (not orange)
Bouncing-Bet	Mullein
Bush clover	Bee-balm
Butter-and-eggs	Pickerelweed
Buttercups	Queen Anne's lace
Cat-tails	Steeplebush
Chicory	Sunflower
Pokeweed	Tansy
Corncockle	Thistle
Daisy	Vetch
Dandelion	Violet (except birdfoot)
Evening-primrose	Yarrow
Everlasting	Camomile
Fireweed	Elder
Goldenrods	Sweetfern
Hawkweed	Hay-scented fern
Ironweed	Lythrum
Miniature mt. cranberry (fruits)	Coneflowers
Salmonberry (fruits)	Gramma and bluestem grasses

Flowers Which May Be Picked in Moderation

Blue-eyed grass
Spring beauty
Eastern-troutlily
Arrowhead
White azalea
Bittersweet
False lily-of-the-valley
Harebell
Blue-flags
Shadbush
American lily-of-the-valley
Coreopsis
Gaillardias
Sundrops
Lupines

Swamp rose-mallow
Sweet pepperbush
Virgin's-bower
Forget-me-not
Yellow pondlily
Groundnut
Sheep-laurel
Wild geranium
Fringed polygala
Yellow wallflowers
Monkey flowers
Mesquites
Acacias
Owl clover

TABLE III

SOIL ACIDITY

In general, most soils with which the wild flower enthusiast is likely to come into contact with will fall under the following headings.

MINIMALKALINE, pH 7-8. Found on limestone ledges, in woods where there is a covering of black leafmold, and in places permeated by lime-carrying waters.

MINIMACID, pH 6-7. A soil of woods, swamps, cultivated fields, and humusy meadows were limestone is prevalent.

CIRCUMNEUTRAL, pH 6-8. This is a broad classification covering the two preceding groups and including soils relished by a large percentage of our garden plants and a fair number of wild flowers.

SUBACID, pH 5-6). Found in old abandoned fields, marshes, upland woods, and meadows lacking limestone.

MEDIACID, pH 4-5. Most characteristic of peat bogs, under coniferous evergreens, in oak forests and rhododendron thickets. Also found in rotting wood, on sand hills and mountain tops where there is no lime. Suitable for trailing arbutus.

SUPERACID, 3-4. Found in some peat bogs, especially where sphagnum moss is the chief ingredient or source of peat. Only a few plants can tolerate it.

Obviously, soil acidity preferences, like other growth factors, vary somewhat. However, the following will serve as a fairly stable guide under normal conditions:

pH 4-5

Chimaphila umbellata cisatlantica
Clintonia borealis
Coptis groenlandica
Cornus canadensis

Lilium philadelphicum
Linnaea borealis americana
Maianthemum canadense
Mitchella repens

Cypripedium acaule
Epigaea repens
Gaultheria procumbens
Habenaria hookeri
Isotria verticillata
Kalmia latifolia
Xerophyllum asphodeloides
Amianthium muscaetoxicum
Phyllodoce empetriformis
Luetkia pectinata
Cassiope mertensiana
Trillium ovatum

Oxalis montana
Rhexia virginica
Rhododendrons
Trientalis borealis
Trillium undulatum
Viola lobata
Pyrola asarifolia
Clintonia uniflora
Erythronium montanum
Anemone occidentale
Loiseleuria procumbens
Empetrum nigrum

pH 5-6

Actaea rubra
Anemone quinquefolia
Anemonella thalictroides
Arisaema triphyllum
Asters
Caltha palustris
Geranium maculatum
Habenaria orbiculata
Habenaria ciliaris
Hepatica americana
Hypoxis hirsuta
Mitella diphylla
Orchis spectabilis
Pedicularis canadensis
Clintonia umbellulata
Orchis spectabilis
Dodecatheon meadia
Solidago misc.

Calypso bulbosa
Chimaphila maculata
Dentaria diphylla
Dicentra eximia
Epilobium angustifolium
Erythronium americanum
Podophyllum peltatum
Polygala paucifolia
Rubus odoratus
Silene virginica
Tiarella cordifolia
Trillium cernuum
Trillium erectum
Trillium decumbens
Dodecatheon jeffreyi
Calochortus nudus
Fritillaria pinetorum

pH 6-8

Actaea pachypoda
Anemone virginiana
Aquilegia canadensis
Arisaema dracontium
Asarum canadense
Camassia scilloides
Cypripedium candidum
Cypripedium calceolus pubescens
Cypripedium reginae
Dentaria laciniata
Dicentra canadensis
Mertensia virginica
Aquilegia caerulea
Trillium pusillum
Trillium stamineum

Trillium grandiflorum
Trillium nivale
Dicentra cucullaria
Erythronium albidum
Geranium robertianum
Hepatica acutiloba
Phlox divaricata
Sanguinaria canadensis
Triphora trianthophora
Uvularia grandiflora
Eschscholzia californica
Clarkia speciosa
Calochortus venustus
Fritillaria pluriflora

In general, most of the plains and desert plants fall into this latter category.

PART TWO

Wild Flowers

WHERE TO FIND THEM AND HOW TO
TRANSPLANT AND GROW THEM

The Anemone Clan—*Anémone and Anemonélla*

Anemonella thalictroídes

Description: Hardy perennials varying in height from 4 to 8 inches in the case of *A. quinquefolia* to 2½ feet or more in *A. virginiana*. The leaves are cut or divided and the flowers are white, buttercup-shaped and are followed by thimble-shaped seed heads on the aneomones.

Where They Grow: As a group, they are denizens of the low, moist areas along the edges of roads and in the more open not-too-dry woodlands over a large part of North America.

Blooming Season: Variable. See individual species below.

Culture: They are, for the most part, easy to handle, making themselves at home in any location to their liking. For individual culture and propagation, see below.

Species: *Anemone canadénsis*—Canada or Meadow Anemone, a 2-foot plant growing from rhizome-like spreading roots, soon forming a large colony. The flowers are single white, 2 inches across, and held above the foliage. The blooming season varies with location, from May to July. Its home is in low moist ground along roadsides and open woods from the Gaspé Peninsula to British Columbia, south to Pennsyvlania, Kansas, and New Mexico and Missouri. Seed sown as soon as ripe often produces blooming plants by the second year whereas spring-sown seed may be dormant a year. It is also propagated by division of the roots in early fall. It is not particular about soil and may spread too much.

A. cylíndrica—Thimble Weed. Frequent in sandy woods and thickets and apparently grows well in moister places too. The tallest of the clan, it grows to nearly 3 feet and seems to like a little more sun. The flowers are creamy, up to 1½ inches across, and appear in early summer, followed by large cone-shaped seed heads full of woolly material. Propagated as above. Maine to Alberta and south to New Jersey, New Mexico, and Arizona. Blooms May to July.

A. deltoídea—A 4 to 12-inch plant with one to several three-parted basal leaves and stalkless leaves above. It is found in the woods of northwestern California to central Washington west of the Cascades but not on the Olympic Peninsula, blooming in April and May.

A. multífida—A little-known species found from Newfoundland to Alaska and south as far as Maine, Vermont, Michigan, and in the mountains to Arizona. It grows from 4 to 12 or 14 inches tall and seems to prefer non-acid, gravelly banks and shores. Try only in the northern or cooler mountain areas.

A. occidentalis—Like *A. nuttalliana*, a strictly western species, it is found in the Sierras, Olympics and Cascades to Alaska and eastward into the northern Rockies. Hairy and 4 to 24 inches tall, it is best known, however, for its large, shaggy, dishmop-like seed head which gives it the common name of old-man-of-the-mountains. It usually prefers open, moist, acid slopes and meadows, blooming early with the glacier lilies, buttercups and spring beauties.

A. parviflóra—Grows about the same size as *A. multifida* and is also a northern species, being found on wet limestone rocks from Newfoundland and Labrador to Minnesota, Colorado, Oregon, and Alaska.

A. quinquefólia—Windflower or Wood Anemone. Small and dainty, only 4 to 8 inches tall, it delights in the moist, acid soil of open woodlands from Nova Scotia to Manibota south to Georgia and Tennessee. Variety *oregana*, with blue or pink sepals, is found from northern California to Washington. The solitary flower is like the others but daintier and is found from April to June. This species is a little more difficult to establish than the others but is a welcome addition to any wild garden. Growing from creeping rootstocks at the tips of which are next year's buds, it is readily propagated by division as soon as the leaves begin to die down and it can also be readily multiplied by seed sown as soon as ripe in pots or flats of light humusy soil.

A. virginiána—Tall Anemone. A plant of the woods, thickets, and clearings from Nova Scotia to Alberta, south to Georgia, Arkansas, and Kansas, it grows 2 to 3 feet tall and blooms June to August. The flowers are scentless, greenish-white, solitary, and up to 1½ inches across. Like the others, the leaves are also divided. Propagation is likewise by seeds and division of the roots preferably when dormant.

Anemonella thalictroídes—While not of the same genus, this plant logically belongs in this group in the public mind. In appearance, it is very much like *Anemone quinquefolia*, being a dainty woods plant with small white (but *not* solitary) flowers on stems 5 to 9 inches tall. In fact, it is found over much the same range (but continues south to Florida and west to Oklahoma) and may even be found in company with it. It is perhaps more easy to establish, however. Propagation is easily accomplished by division of the tiny dahlia-like tubers any time after the foliage has died down or in very early spring. The first fall, especially, top dress the soil with leaf mold to prevent heaving. Seed sown as soon as ripe usually germinates the following spring and produces flowering plants by the second year. Tolerates reasonably acid soil.

A. nuttálliana—Pasque-flower. While this plant is an anemone, it does not belong in the above group. A native from Illinois to Texas, Washington and Alaska, it is a perennial that grows 3 to 6 inches high. The flowers are 2½ inches across, purplish to white (rare) and appear in March to June, before the basal leaves. Another peculiar trait is its habit of noticeably lengthening the stems upon which are found the silky-haired seeds. Propagation is easily accomplished by seeds sown as soon as ripe or in early spring and by division of the roots.

This is the state flower of South Dakota, where it is often mistakenly known as "wild crocus."

holes with water to moisten soil. Carefully lift one
seedling at a time, using the narrowest, thinnest
bladed knife available (such as a cocktail knife),
touching a leaf but not the stem. Let roots drop
into the prepared hole. Cozy the soil against the
roots and tap cup against table surface to settle
the soil. Water with dilute fertilizer solution,
such as 1 tsp. Miracle-Gro to one gallon of tepid
water, promptly.

Keep potted seedlings indoors away from sun one
day, then in a sunny south window or under grow-
lights or outdoors in filtered light, depending upon
the season, until they can be hardened off outdoors
in full sun and a good rootball develops, readying
them for planting. Keep watered!

IV. Planting

Think about the baby plants "mother" sites, and
plan your planting accordingly.

Preferably after a good rain, pull the big weeds
and grasses from your roadside site. Pop the appropriate baby plants out of their Solo Cups and plant them
in the soil you just disturbed. Water promptly with
fertilizer solution (1 Tbsp Miracle-Gro:1 gal. water)
Discourage competition and drying out by mulching
with leaves, woodchips or broken pieces of old shingles,
slanted funnel-style to deliver rainwater the the seedling.

Watch, water and weed area the first year, and
protect with leaf mulch in winter. You've given them
a good start; now your babies are ON THEIR OWN!

Suggestion #1: Have Solo Cups handy when weeding your
garden or lawn, to pot up little volunteer seedlings to
nurture for later planting, after that good rootball
develops.

Suggestion #2: Make your own seedling-flats (also African Violet pots) by filling 2-liter plastic soda bottles with very hot water. In a minute you can twist
off the opaque black or green base, complete with its
own drainage holes.

flats but may need up to 90 days of refrigeration before germinating, the third packet of seed to be strat-
ified. To stratify, prepare the seed for sowing by
putting a few drops of water in the foil seed packet,
seal and place in the freezer section of your refrigerator (not a regular food freezer at 0°F) for several
days, remove for a few hours thawing at room temperature. Repeat twice more, after which seeds are ready
to be sown at your convenience.

II. Starting Seeds

Fill small seedling flats with growing medium to
within ¾" of rim. I use a commercial sterile growing
medium or my own sterilized sifted compost mixed half
and half with clean builder's sand. [Compost can be
sterilized by baking it, moist and foil-covered in a
large baking pan, 30 minutes after an inserted meat
thermometer reaches 180°.]

Soak soil. Drain well. Sprinkle seeds very lightly and evenly over the surface. Cover with a very thin
layer of milled sphagnum moss and spray it with water
until evenly moist. Be sure sphagnum is always moist.
When seedlings appear place in a sunny window or under
grow-lights. [If germinating seeds outdoors, sow seed
on top of a thin layer of fine clean gravel, about ¼"
diameter, washing seeds into crevices with water spray.
The gravel minimizes seed loss through rain splash.]

If seeds need a long period of cool moisture to
germinate, place seedling-flats in plastic bags and re-
frigerate up to 90 days, after soaking, draining and
sowing seed as above. After 4 weeks inspect weekly for
signs of germination, and remove to warmth and light
promptly when leaves appear, after removing plastic bag.

III. Potting Seedlings

Seedlings can be potted in Solo Plastic Cups (with
drainage holes) as soon as they reach the two-true-leaf
stage. Make drainage holes by heating the point of an
icepick over a stove burner until red hot. Then plunge
it into an inverted stack of 8-10 cups three times, making three holes in a triangle. Pull the cups apart
promptly with a twisting motion. Label cups with marker.

Fill cups by dipping into potting soil (commercial,
or your own sterilized compost works well, sifted) and
arranging in a large plastic flat. Using a tableknife
make deep wedge-shaped holes in soil of each cup. Fill

THE SOLO-PLASTIC-CUP WAY
TO ADD COLOR AND INTEREST TO YOUR RURAL ROADSIDE

Why Solo Plastic Cups?

Moisture is retained better in plastic than in paper or peat cups. Potting seedlings in these 3½-oz. cups allows the formation of a large rootball, which pops out easily when planting, makes close contact with surrounding soil and gives the young plant a better chance of surviving the competition of other plants. The cups come in pretty pastel colors, good for color-coding and for labeling with a black Sharpie permanent marker. The cups wash up easily, stack snugly for storage and last through many seasons. Drainage holes are easily made with a red-hot icepick plunged through the base of a stack of ten at a time. The cost at your supermarket is only about 90¢ for a package of 80 cups.

1. Getting Seeds

Watch for colorful or interesting roadside flowers. Return to collect seeds when they have developed.

Keep some Solo Cups in your car, in a plastic bag, with a black Sharpie permanent marker (to record on the cup the kind of seeds collected and the growing conditions at the "mother" site), some plastic sandwich bags to cover the cups, and elastic bands to secure them.

Write to the New England Wild Flower Society, Garden in the Woods, Hemenway Road, Framingham, MA 01701, for their list of sources for native plant seed (The familiar Park Seed Catalogue is listed here, among 32 others), and their own Seed Sale List, and their excellent General Germination Instructions, including the best methods to use on 121 listed plants.

Germination requirements of plants can also be found in the U.S. Department of Agriculture's yearbook on seeds.

If you do not get the germination data, try experimenting. Plan to start a quarter of the freshly collected seeds of a given kind immediately, Nature's way. Dry the rest and store in three packets of folded foil, well labeled: one to be started in small seedling flats in early spring for planting out in May, the second to be started at the same time in seedling

"On the Street Where You Live"

(Lots of little Solo Cups can help you
beautify your rural roadside.)

People often walked down your street before
Never pausing to perceive what Nature had in store,
Now they'll stop and stare at friendly flowers there
Which you've grown for The Street Where You Live.

In the months gone past you've gathered roadside seed,
Then grew baby plants with just the loving care they need,
In cups of yellow, white or blue on which you write
Names and dates and the street where they'll live.

And Oh, the towering feeling
Just to know the method will work!
The Solo Cups with which you are dealing
Have all the attributes to make your efforts work.
They don't dry out as fast;
Through many years they'll last;
Rootballs growing in them pop out ready for the task.

Summer, Fall and Spring, every bloomin' thing
Shows you care for The Street Where You Live.

Educational Exhibit
by Mary Jane Nickerson

At the "Spectrum Musicale" Flower Show
September 28, 1984
The Garden Club of Old Greenwich

The Asters—*Áster*

Description: The asters make up one of the largest groups of wildflowers we have, totaling over 200 species according to some authorities. We cannot hope to treat them all, nor would that be of any advantage since many of them are much alike. We shall discuss only a few best-known or more showy ones.

Asters belong to the composite family. They have flat, daisy-like "flowers," actually many-flowered heads, are hardy long-lived perennials and respond well to cultivation or to release from some of their normal competition. Their colors range from white through pinkish and lavender to blue. The stems are usually tall and the leaves often long and narrow.

Where They Grow: With some exceptions, they are primarily dry-ground plants of the open fields, meadows, and edges of woods, covering the entire continent.

Blooming Season: For the most part, late summer and autumn.

Species: *A. alpigénus*—A dwarf, alpine aster bearing good, pink flowers individually on stems seldom over a foot tall and often less. It inhabits alpine or subalpine rocky or grassy slopes from Washington to California and eastward into the Rockies. It is especially abundant on volcanic peaks such as Mount Rainier and Glacier Peak.

A. cordifólius—Blue Wood or Heart-leaved Aster. One of the latest to bloom, often in October in the latitude of New York. A 2 to 4-foot plant producing numerous pale blue to lavender flowers ½ to ¾ inch across in open woods and under trees in meadows. Roots are shallow and spreading. Common from Nova Scotia to Wisconsin and Georgia.

A. laévis—Smooth Aster. Inhabits dry, sandy soils of open fields and thickets from Maine to Saskatchewan, south to Alabama and Louisiana. Flowers are light violet-blue, an inch across on stems 2 to 4 feet tall. Leaves are stemless, broadly lance-shaped. Blooms late August to October.

A. lateriflórus—Calico Aster. One to 5 feet tall, it is small-flowered, lilac or whitish with magenta-stained stems. Grows in moist or dry soil from Nova Scotia to Minnesota and south to Georgia and Arkansas, August to October.

A. linariifólius—Stiff-leaved Aster. Likes dry hill pastures and sunny banks and rock ledges, usually in acid soil. A small plant (6 to 24 inches) with large violet flowers and stiff, narrow leaves. Improves with cultivation, New Brunswick and Minnesota to the Gulf of Mexico. July to October.

A. modéstus—This is a moderately tall aster, reaching 3½ feet, with a hairy stem, lance-like stalkless leaves and one to numerous heads per stem with 20 to 45 purplish rays each. It blooms July to September in moist woods and along streams from southwest Oregon to Alaska and eastward.

A. nóvae-ángliae—New England Aster, ancestor of many garden varieties. Grows 2 to 5 feet and bears large flowers, rosy-lilac to deep purple. It blooms August to October and does best in deep, rich loam. Does not spread but benefits by division every 2 to 3 years. Common. Easily identified by stickiness and turpentine smell. Quebec to Albera, south to North Carolina and Arkansas.

A. nóvi-bélgi—New York Aster, not an ancestor of garden forms as often claimed. Also likes rich, moist soils. Spreads by creeping roots. Favors more acid soil than the preceding; it is shorter, more branched, and a better blue. Nova Scotia to Ontario, south to Georgia in coastal sphagnum bogs.

A. paucicapitátus—Of modest height, to 20 inches, it is finely downy, leafy-stemmed and the usually 13 rays are white turning to pink. It is native to open slopes at moderate and high altitudes in Washington's Olympic Range.

A. *puníceus*—Swamp Aster. Tall, 2 to 6 feet, with 1-inch lavender blossoms August to October and red or purple stems. Grows anywhere not too dry. Newfoundland to Manitoba, south to Georgia.

A. *spectábilis*—Seaside or Showy Aster. Small, 1 to 2 feet. Fewer but larger blue-violet flowers. Found only along East Coast. One of the best and easy in sandy soil.

Culture: Asters are easily grown. Plant in masses for best results, transplanting in the spring. Propagation is easily accomplished by fall-sown seed (sow thickly, for germination is often poor), division of the crowns in spring, or early summer cuttings rooted in moist sand.

R. canadénse

Description: A large group of woody plants divided by many people into two separate parts, the azaleas which lose their leaves annually, and the rhododendrons which are evergreen. However, the botanists have placed both together under the latter name, since there is no botanical difference in the flowers, and when one gets into the foreign species it is impossible to draw a line between the evergreen and the non-evergreen species.
Where They Grow: See below.
Blooming Season: Spring and summer-blooming, generally May, June, or July, according to species and location.

Species: For the convenience of the readers we shall divide a representative selection into two groups. The first are the "azaleas," the remaining the "rhododendrons."

R. albiflórum—The White Azalea of the Northwest produces flowers along the stem instead of all at the tip. At home on the wet mountain slopes, it is found from Oregon to British Columbia and east into the northern Rockies. It reaches a height of 4 or 5 feet, often forming large thickets.

R. arboréscens—Smooth Azalea. Native to the mountains from Pennsylvania southward, it bears white or pinkish blooms with red stamens in June or July. The flowers are trumpet-like, fragrant, and 2 inches long, but the identifying characteristic is the smoothness of the branchlets and the leaves which are shining above and glaucous beneath.

R. atlánticum—Coast Azalea. A dwarf plant reaching a height of 2 feet, it spreads by means of suckers. The fragrant, white or pinkish flowers generally appear before the leaves. Native from South Carolina to Delaware.

R. canadénse—Rhodora. A small shrub rarely growing over 3 or 4 feet tall, the flowers a purplish-rose, narrower-petaled and less trumpet-like. The flowers generally appear well before the leaves and color the cool bogs and wet slopes from Newfoundland to Quebec, south to New Jersey and Pennsylvania.

R. canéscens—Hoary Azalea. Like most of the species described here, it grows 3 to 10 feet high and is often confused with the other pink-flowered species. However, the leaves are wider and shorter than those of the pinxter described below. Found in the woods and swamps from Delaware to Florida, Ohio, and East Texas. April and May.

R. calenduláceum—Flame Azalea. The most striking of the group, it is native from the Catskill region of New York southward through the mountains to Georgia and Alabama, but under cultivation will grow noticeably farther north. Variable in color, the flowers may be anywhere from orange-red to yellow, but lack fragrance.

R. camtscháticum—Kamchatka Rhododendron is a small semi-deciduous shrub of about 8 inches, bearing solitary or paired flowers of rose-purple. Native

49

to northeast Asia, Alaska and British Columbia, it can also be grown in suitable rock gardens on the East Coast.

R. *nudiflórum*—Pink Azalea, Pinxter-Flower, the best known of the native azaleas and perhaps the most confused, being commonly lumped with R. *vaseyi, roseum,* and *canescens* in the average person's mind. The nearly odorless flowers appear before the leaves are fully expanded and are pink or occasionally varying to white, trumpet-shaped, up to 1½ inches across and hairy on the outside. The leaves are pointed at both ends and hairy on the principal veins and mid-rib beneath. A showy, easily-grown species generally found in moist sandy or rocky woods or around the borders of bogs and swamps from Massachusetts and Ohio to South Carolina and Tennessee.

R. *occidentále*—Western Azalea. Well known as a deciduous shrub reaching 10 feet or more on stream banks and moist flats, often in partial shade, from southern California to southern Oregon. The white or pink-flushed flowers appear from May to July according to location.

R. *róseum*—Early Azalea. For our purposes, it is similar to the above but has a delightful clove-like fragrance—the sweetest of all the spring shrubs—and is far more worthy of culture and preservation than R. *nudiflorum.* Maine to Quebec, south to Virginia and Missouri, in woods, thickets, and rocky banks.

R. *váseyi*—The Pinkshell Azalea. Because of its erect habit and very free flowering, it is a most attractive species, but unfortunately is confined in nature only to parts of North Carolina. However, it has found its way into the nursery trade and may be readily purchased from a number of nurserymen. The flowers vary from white to rose and the leaves turn a good crimson in the autumn. Found in woods, peaty banks, and ravines where it gets sun part of the day.

R. *viscósum*—Clammy or White Swamp Azalea. This one is sometimes confused with the smooth azalea, but the branchlets are bristly as well as the margins and the mid-ribs of the otherwise smooth leaves. It is found in swamps from Maine to the Carolinas and west to Ohio and Tennessee. The flowers appear June to August, are white or pinkish and sticky on the outside. Since the flowers appear after the leaves are out, the plant is not so showy as some species.

R. *minus*

/————/

R. *caroliniánum*—Carolina Rhododendron, a more slender plant with smaller leaves and flowers than the better-known R. *catawbiense* and *maximum* below. A plant of the more or less open uplands, it is native to the Blue Ridge Mountains. The flowers are usually light rose pink but may vary to white. A fast grower from seed after the first few months.

R. *catawbiénse*—Catawba Rhododendron or Mountain Rosebay, the best known of the native rhododendrons, grows anywhere from 3 to 20 feet tall and bears great trusses of up to 20 blooms, each 1½ to 2½ inches across, the first week in June in the latitude of New York. A native of the upper slopes and summits of the Alleghenies from Virginia to Georgia, it is dependably hardy even in full sun and well up into New England.

R. *macróphyllum* (or *macrophýllum*)—California or Washington Rosebay is the state flower of Washington. Pink-flowered, it inhabits the moist, acid soils (though drier than R. *albiflorum*). Coastal in British Columbia and Washington, it jumps to the Cascades in Oregon and northern California. More than twice the height of the white azalea, it is evergreen.

R. *máximum*—Rosebay. Well-known and readily obtained from nurserymen. It is native in low woods and along streams from Quebec southward but rare except in the mountains from Pennsylvania to Georgia. Taller-growing but shyer-blooming, it also prefers a partially shaded location. The flowers are rose-pink to white and appear in July in the vicinity of New York.

R. *mínus*—Like a large Carolina, but it blooms later and the color is deeper. From the sandy woods of the inner coastal plain and lower mountains, North Carolina to Alabama. Hardy at least to Southern New England.

R. *lappónicum*—Lapland Rosebay. A low, creeping shrub often less than 12 inches high. The flowers are ¾ inch in diameter, rosy to purplish and somewhat bell-shaped. Found only on alpine summits, New York, New Hampshire, and Maine as well as Alaska and the sub-Arctic. Not easily grown except under like conditions.

Culture: All like a peaty, well-drained soil, even those which grow in moist places. While some are found on limestone rocks, a close check usually shows the soil to be acid. Propagation is readily effected by careful division of large clumps, accompanied by cutting back the tops to 6 to 12 inches when the plants are not in active growth, as late summer or very early spring. Layering can also be practiced. However, when time permits, growing from seed is best for producing plants in large quantities—collecting plants from the wild should be discouraged, except in the path of construction.

Seed should be sown when ripe in flats of peatmoss and sand, barely covered with fine sphagnum, and placed in a coldframe. Keep it moist, watering only from the bottom or with a fine spray. When large enough, transplant to light, sandy, peaty soil in flats and again to lath-shaded frames. Leaf-cutting propagation is also possible but not for amateurs.

The newer method of air layering using sheet plastic is also effective for small quantities.

The Baneberries—*Actaéa*

A. rúbra

Description: Interesting plants noted more for their fruits than their flowers. Perennials, they grow from 1 to 2 feet tall and produce gracefully divided leaves from branching stems. The flowers are small, white, feathery and borne in dense terminal clusters. They are not particularly showy and, in general, remind one somewhat of false Solomon's seal. The fruits are oval, stalked, and mature about September.

Where They Grow: Natives of the rich woods and thickets, the red baneberries are at home from Labrador west to British Columbia and Alaska, south to New Jersey, Ohio, Colorado, and Oregon. The white is scarcer in the northern part of its range which extends from Prince Edward's Island to Manitoba, south to Florida, Louisiana, and Oklahoma.

Blooming Season: April to June according to location.

Species: There are two principal species:

A. *pachýpoda* (A. *álba.*)—Long a favorite with the children because each half-inch, oval white berry which grows on a short, thick reddish stem has a blackish "eye" opposite the stem end and is responsible for the common name "dolls' eyes." As a rule, it prefers slightly deeper woods than the following and ripens its fruits from 1 to 3 weeks later.

A. *rúbra*—Similar to the above but bearing bright red fruits without such prominent "eyes" on more slender stems.

Culture: Given shade and a rich, woodsy soil with a reasonably good supply of moisture, baneberries are very easy to grow and, once established, are among the most permanent of wild flowers.

They are easily grown from seed. Sow the flattish, horizontally-packed seeds as soon as ripe—simply mashing the berries gently between the fingers—in pots of light, humusy soil plunged into a coldframe or into the open soil in a sheltered place out of doors. Cover lightly with peatmoss or similar material to prevent drying out. They should come up the following spring and bloom by the third year. If the seeds dry out, they may take a year longer to germinate.

For best results, transplant to individual pots, plant bands or outside 3 to 5 inches apart each way as soon as they are large enough to handle, and give more room as necessary.

They can also be propagated by division of the roots in late fall or early spring. Given a soil with an acidity rating of 5 to 6 for red baneberries and 6 to 7 for the white, they will be particularly at home in the wild garden with maidenhair and shield ferns as well as wild geraniums and false lily-of-the-valley.

Bearberry—*Arctostáphylos úva-úrsi*

Description: One of our finest and most desirable evergreen groundcovers. The small leaves are oval, alternate, about an inch long, rather thick, glossy and take on an attractive bronzy tone in the fall. The flowers, on the other hand, are tiny, white or pinkish, and are not borne too plentifully, but they give way to shining red berries which are about the size of currants (¼ inch in diameter) and persist through the winter, furnishing welcome food for the game birds.

In habit, the bearberry is a low, creeping woody-stemmed shrub trailing over the ground and rooting at the joints as it goes. In its younger stages it often appears to be a slow-growing plant but when well established and happy in its location it can spread as much as 2 feet a year.

Where They Grow: Bearberries are denizens of the dry, sandy areas and rocky or gravelly banks south to Virginia, Montana, and California to Alaska. Typical of their habitat are the sandy stretches of Cape Cod and the pine barrens of New Jersey. Another closely related, but black-fruited sort, *A. alpína*, inhabits Alaska and the Far North, coming as far south as the mountain tops of Maine and New Hampshire in the East. Other red and brown-fruited species are found on the coast and in the mountains of California, etc.

Blooming Season: May or June.

Culture: Given a gravelly, sandy soil with good drainage, full sun or part shade, and the company of oaks, gray birches, pines and low-bush blueberries, the bearberry will last for many years, becoming larger and more beautiful every season. However, it is not a subject that transplants readily from the wild, unless it is possible to find young plants and move them with a large sod—not an easy task in sandy soil. Consequently, it is best to make a start with pot-grown plants from some nurseryman. From then on the plants can be increased as one wishes.

Seed taken from the berries as soon as ripe may be sown ½ to ¾ inch deep in flats of sand and peatmoss and kept outdoors all year round, but germination is slow, often taking from 2 to 5 years. Storing several months in moist sand and peat in a refrigerator at about 40° will often speed up germination somewhat. Another method is to soak the seeds for 4 or 5 hours in sulphuric acid in an earthen container before planting. This will often result in a fair germination the first year.

A better method of propagation is to take cuttings 3 to 5 inches long, in July, of the new wood with a heel of the older wood attached. Then plunge them halfway down into sand to which a little peat has been added and keep moist. They should be rooted by spring. If one has a greenhouse available, hardwood cuttings may be taken in fall or winter and rooted indoors. If desired, a rooting hormone for woody plants may be used.

Bitter-root—*Lewísia redivíva*

Description: A low, somewhat fleshy-leaved perennial named for Captain Lewis of the famous Lewis and Clark Expedition to the Northwest after the Louisiana Purchase. Perhaps it would be better to call it a stemless perennial with a rosette of narrowly oblong leaves about an inch long growing from the top of a carrot-like fleshy root.

The flowers are borne singly at the tops of low stems that rise but little above the leaves, are 2 inches across, and look like wheels with their 8 to 15 pink or occasionally white petals. They open with the coming of the sun each day and close toward evening over a long period.

Although a true Westerner, it has no objections to life in the East, being extremely hardy even in the coldest areas. What has probably led to some misunderstandings regarding its longevity and permanence is its habit of making its leaf growth in the fall, the dying of the leaves with the coming of the flowers in late spring and its complete disappearance in summer. In fall, when cooler weather and rains arrive, it comes to life again.

Where They Grow: Native to dry places, it is particularly at home in Montana, Wyoming, Utah, and west to the Pacific.

Blooming Season: Spring, generally April or May.

Other Species: Popular with rock gardeners is *L. cotylédon* from California and Oregon, a similar but easier grower elsewhere. Another is the pale peach to white *L. tweédyi* from the Wenatchee Mountains.

Culture: As we have just said, it is very hardy even in the coldest areas. It does well in dry, rocky, well-drained places with some humus, especially if given full sun. Also, it is best when planted in groups on a sun-baked hillside, where it can send its fleshy roots sprawling beneath the stones. If the situation does not already exist, mix in plenty of sand and pebbles or stone chips more than a foot to ensure the plants getting a good start.

Transplanting, of course, is best done carefully and while the plants are still dormant in the early fall, although young growing plants may be set out in the spring, too. With respect to their longevity out of the soil it is interesting to note that the plants from which it was first described were discovered to still show signs of life after having been in the herbarium for several years. The botanist Pursh noted this and planted them—and they grew for a year—resulting in the species name *redivíva!* Any way you look at it, the lewisia is a plant well worthy of preservation in its natural state for future generations, as well as in private and public collections.

Propagation: The best method, by far, is to grow them from seed. Further, the seedlings move better and adapt themselves to new locations more easily than older plants. The one hitch is that the seed is hard to collect. As soon as it is ripe, a joint below the seed heads breaks, the seeds drop and blow away. For spring sowing first store the seed 3 to 4 weeks or longer in slightly moist sand at 38 to 40°. Then fill a flat with 1 part leafmold and 2 parts coarse sand, first putting in a layer of peat or chopped sphagnum. Top with the mixture finely screened. Scatter the seed and cover lightly by sifting a little more mixture over it. Moisten by setting the flat into a pan of water when necessary and transplant into other flats, or better, pots or plant bands as soon as the seedlings begin to crowd one another. Do not attempt to set out into the wild until the spring of the second year.

Black-eyed Susan—*Rudbéckia hírta*

Description: Upon first thought, the well-known black-eyed Susan of our fields needs no description. Yet, it is one of a fairly large group of somewhat similar plants. So, a few comments may be in order. Like all *Rudbeckias*, its flowers are daisy-like with a fairly high central disc, and its leaves are alternate. (*Heliopsis*, for instance, are opposite and *Helianthus* often so.)

The 10 to 15 orange-yellow rays are long and curl backward, while the tiny disc flowers are dark brown. Both stems and lanceolate leaves are rough and covered with stiff hairs.

Where They Grow: Usually in grassy places such as fields or open woods even where the soil is poor. Primarily a mid-westerner, it spread with the cutting of the forests until it now covers most of the United States and adjoining Canada and Mexico.

Blooming Season: June to August.

Other Species: Of the 18 other species it might also be well to touch upon at least a few of the better known ones.

R. califórnica—A tall species blooming in July and August in moist meadows in the southern Sierras. Perennial.

R. laciniáta—Tall or Green-headed Coneflower. Best-known as the original single-flowered parent of the familiar goldenglow of old-fashioned gardens. A tall, leafy, much-branched perennial 8 to 10 feet or more high with thin, comparatively smooth leaves cut into 3 to 7 parts. The flowers are yellow and centered with tall, greenish-yellow discs. Blooms July to September and is generally found in moist thickets and low woods, especially near streams, from Quebec to Manitoba, south to Florida and Texas.

R. tríloba—Thin-leaved Coneflower. Similar to *R. hirta* but more branched and with smaller flowers—2 inches across. It grows 2 to 5 feet tall with rough but not hairy stems. The leaves are thin, bright green, and rough, the lower 3-lobed, the upper broader than *R. hirta's*. A native of open woods and fields in both moist and drier soils, it is found from New England to Minnesota, south to Georgia, Arkansas, and Oklahoma. Blooms August.

Culture: While these plants are not so much in need of conservation and may be picked freely, there are roadsides and other areas where a few might well be naturalized. Some species are biennials and, therefore, useless to move as grown plants. Grow them from seed which is produced freely. Sow it as soon as ripe in flats in a coldframe or in outside beds like garden flowers. Move to the wild at the end of the first year's growth.

R. californica and *laciniáta* are more reliably perennial and can be propagated by division.

Bloodroot—*Sanguinária canadénsis*

Description: One of our best-known wild flowers, the bloodroot is to many just as much the symbol of spring as the trailing arbutus. A sturdy, reliable plant with a fragile flower, the bloodroot comes up year after year, making larger and sturdier clumps. As they break through the ground in early spring, each tightly-rolled leaf encloses a flower bud, keeping it safe from harm as they force their way upward through the soil. Then as the leaf slowly begins to unroll, the flower stem pushes up the bud beyond the leaf where it opens into a graceful bloom. The glistening white petals, usually 8 in number, are long and elliptic. They open flat in the morning, are erect by late afternoon, and close in the evening.

The leaves which are more or less rounded and divided into (usually 7) shallow and irregular or "chewed-out looking" lobes, are blue-olive green and make a handsome foil for the delicate white flowers. Eventually the leaves expand until just before they disappear for the year, they are 8 to 10 inches across and about as high.

The fruit is a narrow, one-celled capsule which is about 1 inch long and pointed at each end. The common name, of course, comes from the stout, horizontal rootstock which is ½ to 1 inch thick and, like the stems, is full of a red juice once used by the Indians as a dye and by the whites for many years on sugar as a cough remedy.

Where They Grow: Along shaded lanes and in rich woods from the maritime provinces to Manitoba, south to Kentucky, Illinois, and Kansas. (*Var. rotundifolia:* Florida and Texas, north to New York and Wisconsin).

Blooming Season: Generally April or May.

Culture: Although an excellent wild garden plant which should have a place in every wooded preserve, park, nature trail, or home sanctuary, it is distinctly not a plant for picking. Alone, the flowers lose much of their grace and the petals soon fall, making their picking a senseless waste.

Although moving is possible at other seasons, late fall is best, for then the plants are dormant but about to throw out new roots in preparation for the next spring's growth and bloom.

Give them a rich, humus-filled soil, slightly moist and in partial shade with a pH of 6 to 7 (just barely acid). Apparently deciduous woods (especially those predominantly maple), are preferred.

Propagation may be effected with seeds sown as soon as ripe in pots or flats in a coldframe. Protect from mice with screen, glass, or plastic film. Use a light shady, humusy soil covered with at least ½ inch of finely shredded sphagnum moss to check damping off. Germination will take place the following spring and blooming may start the year after that.

Slower in number of new plants but faster in time is division of the roots when the plants begin to die down in late summer.

For those who are interested, there is also a double-flowered form obtainable from some native plant nurserymen. The flowers last longer than those of normal form.

The Bluebells—*Campánula*

C. rapunculoídes

Description: A large group of plants, several of which are native to North America. While they vary greatly in size and general appearance, all have 5-lobed bell-like flowers which give way to pods opening on the sides and alternate or nearly alternate leaves.

Where They Grow: See below.

Blooming Season: See below.

Species: *C. americána*—An annual growing 2 to 5 feet tall. The leaves are large, thin, dark green, ovate to ovate-lance-shaped and somewhat drooping. The flowers are about 1 inch across, deeply cleft, pale blue to whitish and appear in a terminal spike. Blooms June to August. In moist, rich soil New York to Ontario, south to Florida and Missouri, but not well-known.

C. aparinoídes—Bedstraw Bellflower. A small perennial with slender, weak stems 6 to 20 inches long and narrow leaves ½ to 1½ inches long. The flowers are ⅓ inch across on stems diverging widely from the main stem. Usually white, common in grassy swamps, flowering June to August. Canada to Georgia, west to Kentucky and Colorado.

C. párryi—a 10-inch species that blooms in July and August in moist meadows in Washington's Wenatchees and east into Idaho, Montana and Utah. Perennial.

C. rapunculoídes—European Bellflower. An import, widely naturalized from Newfoundland to the Dakotas, south to Ohio and Missouri. Produces a simple, erect stem up to 3 feet. The upper leaves are thin and lance-shaped, the lower more arrow-like. The flowers are purplish-blue and hang downward, mostly on one side of the stem and remain in bloom over a long period in July or August. A perennial, it will readily take care of itself.

C. rotundifólia—Bluebell. One of the daintiest and most delicate-appearing campanulas, yet one of the hardiest. A perennial, it withstands life on open, rocky banks, shores and mountain tops from Labrador to Alaska, south to New Jersey, Nebraska, California and Arizona. (Also in Europe and Asia.) The name refers to the tuft of small round leaves in the spring. Before flowering, these wither and are replaced by slender wiry 4- to 18-inch stems bearing linear leaves and graceful violet-blue bells July to September. In the fall new basal leaves appear.

Culture: American campanulas are comparatively easy. All can be grown from seed sown in a mixture of coarse sand with a little loam and peatmoss, as soon as ripe and transplanted as necessary. Give good drainage, with plenty of gravel, in neutral to slightly acid reasonably moist soil.

C. rapunculoides also propagates from creeping rootstocks or division almost any time. *C. rotundifolia* can also be grown from root cuttings in sandy loam in September as well as top cuttings taken the same time and rooted in sand. Winter both seedlings and cuttings in a protected coldframe. Do not feed.

Bunchberry or Dwarf Dogwood—*Córnus canadénsis*

Description: A tiny cousin of the dogwood tree and one of our finest ground covers when conditions are to its liking. From a mass of slender perennial rootstocks creeping around just under the surface of the soil grow numerous 4- to 8-inch stiffly upright stems, each bearing, usually, 6 toothless broadly ovate leaves arranged in a whorl at its top. Then, in the center from which these leaves radiate there grows what appears to be a simple 4-petaled white flower but which is really composed of 4 white bracts and a collection of tiny, inconspicuous flowers in the center. When these are gone, their place is taken by clusters of vivid red berries which last well into the winter, if not eaten by birds.

Where They Grow: They inhabit the cool, rich open woods where the soil is acid (pH 4.5) and damp, from Labrador to Alaska south to California, New Mexico, Minnesota, Indiana, West Virginia, and New Jersey as well as northeast Asia.

Blooming Season: May to July depending upon the latitude and exposure to the sun, followed by berries which last many months.

Culture: Boon companion to the clintonias, oxalis, false lily-of-the-valley, painted trilliums, blueberries and mountain cranberries, it will not grow unless the soil is acid, full of humus, cool and damp. However, if these conditions are met and shade provided, it will make itself completely at home and spread rapidly. The best way to transplant it, especially for reestablishing it in parks, wild flower preserves, etc., is to chop out sods intact. Then water well and mulch with peatmoss or pine needles to prevent drying out.

Propagation may be accomplished by sowing the seed, removed from the berries, in flats in a coldframe or protected spot in the open, before they dry out. Cover ½ to ¾ inch deep. Germination usually takes place the following spring and the plants reach blooming size the third year.

Another way is to pull a sod apart, pot up the runners in the sandy, acid soil in late summer, and carry the plants over winter in a coldframe, never letting them get too dry. They should be ready for planting out by late spring. In any case, whether from seeds or cuttings, pot-grown plants are easier to manage and can be set out almost any time of the year.

An excellent groundcover and a plant well worth taking steps to preserve for future generations. Let us all do our part with this and our other wild flowers.

Buttefly Weed—*Asclépias tuberósa*

Description: By far the handsomest of all the milkweeds, it is also one of the easiest of all the wildflowers to handle. A hardy, long-lived perennial, the buttefly weed grows from a thick tuberous root that penetrates to great depths. The leaves are narrowly oblong and not noteworthy but the large flat-topped clusters of brilliant orange flowers are truly spectacular and can be seen a long way off. Another attractive feature is the large number of butterflies they attract all the time they are in bloom. After the flowers are gone, their place is taken by pairs of curious beak-like pods that eventually open and release numerous silk-plumed seeds. The usual height is 1 to 2 feet. Unlike most other members of the clan, these plants contain little milk.

Where They Grow: Common in dry fields, gravelly banks, roadsides and along railroad embankments where their thick, fleshy roots enable them to survive. Their range is from Maine to Florida and west to North Dakota, Ontario and northern Mexico.

Blooming Season: Generally June through August, although occasionally the blooming may continue on into September in some areas.

Other Species: While there are many other members of this clan, none compare with *A. tuberosa* for showiness:

A. amplexicaúlis—A lilac-flowered plant also of the dry waste places.

A. incarnáta—Swamp Milkweed. Purplish-pink flowers. Often found with Joe-Pye-Weed. Good around pools or water courses.

A. purpuráscens—Purple Milkweed. Another dry-land plant with showy magneta blooms.

A. quadrifólia—Four-leaved Milkweed. Leaves in 4's around the stem instead of in pairs; flowers lilac pink. Prefers rich loam in more or less damp woods.

Culture: Because of their far-reaching roots butterfly weeds are difficult to transplant. However, that should not deter anyone from growing them either in the wild garden or the not-so-wild garden—they readily make themselves at home in the average perennial border, too, provided the soil is not too heavy. In heavy soils they often winter-kill. Give them full sun and perfect drainage.

Propagation is easy. Seed sown in the fall will often produce blooming plants the following season. Growth is rather rapid and transplanting them to their permanent homes before the first year is over usually produces better results unless they are grown in large pots to make transplanting easier.

Root cuttings 1½ to 2 inches long, taken in early May and set upright just beneath the surface in a sandy soil, root readily—much more readily than when laid horizontally—if kept slightly moist.

Butterwort and Burnet—*Pinguícula vulgáris* and *Sanguisórba canadénsis*

Two more plants discussed together simply for convenience.

Description: Small plants 4 to 8 inches high, pinguiculas are often confused with violets. However, unlike violets, their 5 petals are united into a tube and the stamens number only 2. The leaves are shining, "painted with butter" to some, which accounts for the name, and they exude a sticky juice which catches and digests minute insects like the other carnivorous plants.

Where They Grow: Generally found on wet banks, moss-covered rocks or in bogs, Newfoundland to Alaska and south to New England, New York, Minnesota and Washington State.

Blooming Season: June to early August.

Culture: Interesting and unusual little plants, but they must have the proper surroundings to succeed. The best place is in the mosses and thin soil among the rocks near a stream or waterfall where the air is cool and moist and no deep, rich soil. Even when found over limestone rocks their neighbors are almost sure to be acid-lovers like spruces, bunchberries, *Kalmia polifolia*, and dwarf potentillas.

Seeds are produced freely and offsets from the base of the plant. The latter may be separated and grown as individual plants. Either way, they can be raised in a mixture of leafmold or peat and a little sand in pots like African violets until ready to set out. The photo was taken on the West Coast of Newfoundland.

/———/

Description: If you see a slender, erect plant 1 to 3, or even 5 feet high, with leaves like mountain ash but daintier and not so pointed and whitish heads that in a rough way remind one of timothy grass, that is *Sanguisorba* or burnet.

Where They Grow: Generally in acid peaty or boggy soils in marshes, meadows, or the edges of streams and ponds from eastern Canada to Michigan, south to Delaware and in the mountains to Georgia.

Blooming Season: Midsummer until autumn.

Culture: A plant of the moist, often boggy, places, generally in full sun. A perennial, it can be increased by division in fall or spring and by seeds sown in pots of moist, sandy-peaty soil. Give more room when necessary and set out the second year. A plant well worth saving.

Camass Lilies—*Camássia scilloídes (C. esculénta)* and Relatives

Description: A slender plant, somewhat like the large garden scillas in appearance but taller and with a longer spike. The long, narrow leaves also resemble those of the hemerocallis and grow directly from an onion-like bulb, while the light blue, star-like flowers are borne on simple racemes up to 18 inches high. Blooming starts at the bottom and works upward, usually lasting a fairly long time.

Where They Grow: The only true eastern species, it prefers the rich soil of damp mostly sunny meadows from Pennsylvania to Wisconsin and south to Alabama and Texas.

Blooming Season: Usually in May except in the southern portions of its range where it comes into bloom earlier.

Other Species: Since it is within the province of this book, it seems advisable to also discuss the western species, since they are much more showy and will grow satisfactorily even in the East.

C. cúsicki—Cusick's Camass. A rather scarce and less-known species from the Snake River region of eastern Oregon but worth planting even on the East Coast. The bulbs are as large as small potatoes and send up more and wider leaves than the other species. The flower stem is about 3 feet tall, strong, erect, and the flowers are a pale blue-lavender.

C. leíchtlini—Leichtlin's Camass. Also a stronger power than its eastern cousin, it sometimes reaches a height of 3 to 4 feet. The flowers are deep blue to lavender and a white variety is also known. This is, perhaps, the best western species for planting outside its normal range. Two methods of identification— the seed pods stand away from the stalks and often have the withered petals still clinging twisted to them until the seeds are ripe. For best effect it should be planted in groups. Sierras and Coast Ranges, California to Canada.

C. quámash—Often confused with *C. scilloídes* since both improperly bore that name while the latter was also known as *C. fraseri* or *hyacinthina*. Native from British Columbia to California and east to Montana, Utah and Wyoming, it produces a spike 30 inches tall or more and blooms in May. The flowers are large, widely expanded and a lustrous purple-blue. In this species the seed pods are erect. While all are edible, this is the one whose bulbs were most favored by the Indians. Today there are fewer plants because the bulbs were so used for years.

Culture: All the camassias are comparatively easy to grow, even on the East Coast. They are hardy, not fussy about soils, although they appear to prefer ones that are neutral or only slightly acid. While in the wild state they are sometimes found in wet meadows where water stands in winter and early spring, it is not necessary. In fact, it does not appear desirable when growing them out of the normal range. They do best in a fairly rich, loamy soil and even withstand some drought in summer. The bulbs should be planted in the fall—mature ones not over 4 inches deep, younger ones less.

While the bulbs rarely produce offsets unless wounded, they can be easily propagated for stocking areas from seeds which germinate readily and soon fill the flat with their grassy foliage.

Carolina Thermopsis and Moth Mullein
Thermópsis caroliniána and Verbáscum blattária

Description: Large yellow pea-like flowers growing on tall delphinium-like plants is what the Carolina thermopsis looks like at first glance. Being a true legume, it has typical legume flowers but there is nothing low or dainty about the plant. It grows 3 to 5 feet tall, producing long spires of these attractive golden blooms above shapely plants covered with pea-like, 3-parted slightly grayish-green leaves.

Where They Grow: Native in the edges of woods and open places, often in poor, dryish soils from the Carolinas to Georgia.

Blooming Season: June or July in most places.

Culture: Why this plant should be so little-known either in the wild or in gardens —for it also makes a good plant for the perennial flower border—is a mystery to me. Granted its range is small, but it readily adapts itself almost anywhere, even in the most northern and western states. In its native region, it is generally known as Aaron's rod.

It will grow in full sun or light shade, likes deep, well-drained soils, but will survive on poor, dry ones. For establishing itself on hot dry hillsides and sandy places it has few equals among the more showy plants and is one which might well be naturalized on road cuts and rough places wherever such a plant would be appropriate.

Propagation is possible by division, but old plants are deep-rooted and the use of seeds is easier. It is also better for large scale production of plants. Sow outside in a prepared bed as soon as ripe. Seedlings usually appear in spring. Transplant as necessary and set out permanently their second spring.

/———/

Description: Not a native but a welcome addition to our flora, this European immigrant makes an attractive plant 2 to 6 feet tall. Its general outline is like that of its close relative, the common woolly mullein, but is more slender and graceful. Likewise, it lacks the woolliness. The flowers are large, about an inch across, white or pale yellow tinged with lavender on the back and much farther apart on the 1 to 2 foot raceme than those of its woolly cousin.

Where They Grow: Dryish fields and waste places where few other attractive plants grow from New England to Ontario, south and west over most of the United States. Usually in full sun.

Blooming Season: June to September according to location with flowering lasting several weeks in any one place.

Culture: Their culture is easy. Give them full sun and almost anything for soil except a wet one. Since they are biennials, seed is the only practical means of propagation. Empty the seeds from the roundish capsules as soon as ripe and sow outdoors in any reasonably well-prepared bed with good drainage. They germinate in the spring and are ready to be set out at the end of the first season into locations where it is desired that they naturalize themselves. Do so two years in succession to ensure flowering-sized plants each year.

Clintonia, Blue Beads—*Clintónia boreális, etc.*

Description: In spite of their relatively inconspicuous flowers, these are plants well worth preserving. From a slender perennial rootstock it throws up 2 to 5 (usually 3) thickish, handsome, shining leaves somewhat similar in shape to those of the pink ladyslipper but much smoother. From early spring to well into the fall they remain fresh, green, and attractive. They measure 6 to 8 inches long and 2 to 3 inches wide.

The 3 to 6 flowers usually appear in a loose cluster rising a foot or more above the leaves on a leafless stem. They are bell-like, 1 inch long, greenish yellow, and give way to large, dark blue, shining, nearly round fruits that look just like the old-fashioned clay marbles.

Where They Grow: Typical plants of the cool, moist northern woods, they grow in damp, shaded places from Labrador to Manitoba and south through the mountains to Georgia. In the more southern portions of their range they often prefer the cooler, moister northern slopes.

Blooming Season: Late May through June or later, according to geographical and immediate location, the berries appearing June through August.

Other species: *C. andréwsiana*—Usually has five or six leaves, red or purplish flowers in a cluster and blue berries. Native to the Coast Ranges of middle California to southwest Oregon, preferring damp woods.

C. umbellulàta—The White Clintonia is a more southern species, being found in rich woods of New York and Ohio and in the Alleghenies to Georgia. Its flowers are smaller, a speckled white, and are borne in a thick, upright cluster instead of nodding. The stem is also inclined to be woolly and the berries nearly black. It seems to require a somewhat less acid soil and not so cool and moist a location. Otherwise its wants are similar.

C. uniflóra—The one (or two) white flowers are borne above two or three leaves May to July. At home in shaded woods in California's Sierras and north to Canada as well as east to Montana.

Culture: As stated above, *C. borealis* needs a cool, humus-filled, acid soil averaging about pH 5, good drainage, and a steady supply of moisture. Among its preferred companions are false lily-of-the-valley, trilliums, troutlilies, bunchberries, and oxalis in the shade of hemlock-maple-beech woods or the northern evergreens such as firs and spruces.

Propagation may be effected by removing the pulp from the berries and planting the seeds as soon as ripe to produce blooming size plants in 2 to 3 years. A slower method is division in late fall.

Transplanting is not difficult if one will remember that in late summer, each year, the parent plant puts out one or more underground runners several inches in length and at the end of each is a bud for next year's growth. Then the parent plant dies and if the buds were not taken, too, there will be no plants the following year. For best results mulch with leaves the first winter, at least, if nature hasn't done it for you, and help save these plants so that others may enjoy them, too.

The Columbines—*Aquilégia canadénsis, etc.*

Description: the columbines easily rank among the most graceful and beautiful of American wild flowers. The pendant red and yellow "bells" with their 5 long spurs pointing jauntily upward dance in every breeze, while the finely divided foliage is much like that of the anemones and the meadow rue. It grows to a height of 12 to 24 inches and is one of our hardiest plants. Growing from thick, deep-seated, perennial rootstocks, plants may last many years.

Where They Grow: From Nova Scotia to Canada's Northwest Territory and south to Georgia and Texas, the Canada columbine may be found on dryish banks and rocky ledges in full sun or the part shade late April through May.

Other Species: As an escape from cultivation one also occasionally sees the squattier but longer-spurred blooms of the European columbine, *A. vulgaris*, with its flowers of blue, purple, pink or white.

From Colorado and adjoining territory comes the equally attractive blue and white *A. caerúlea*, its state flower. It is not at all difficult.

A. chrysántha—A tall, handsome yellow from moist places in Colorado and into the Southwest. Blooms April to September in woods and canyons.

A. elegántula—Another red and yellow species, it is shorter than the following and little flaring. Native to rocky and wooded slopes, Utah, Colorado and New Mexico and southward:

A. formósa—20 to 40 inches tall, widespread and variable, its flowers are widely flaring and red and yellow. From moist woods, southern California to Alaska, Utah and Montana. *A. eximia* from moist places in the Coast Ranges of California are rather similar in form and somewhat in color.

A. pubéscens—Has erect flowers, white with pale pink spurs. Grows in high, rocky places in the southern Sierras of California.

Culture: It grows readily in almost any soil but seems to prefer one with an acidity rating of about 6. The thing to guard against is too rich a soil. Under such conditions it grows too vigorously and tends to become short-lived as well as coarse. With care it may be moved in late fall or early spring but the deep rootstock makes this difficult except with young plants.

However, it is very readily propagated from seed sown as soon as ripe and is one of the few wild flowers that can be increased by merely scratching the seed into the soil where they are wanted to grow. Nevertheless, sowing in pots or flats in a coldframe or a sheltered bed, transplanting when large enough and again later, is preferable. Such plants become much better established in the wild— they usually flower the following spring and establish a permanent colony sooner. Under normal conditions columbines self-sow freely.

COLOR PLATES

Color photographs by Paul Martin Brown (1–15), New England Wild Flower Society (16), Mrs. Eugene H. Walker (17–21), Edwin F. Steffek (22–38), and Edwin F. Steffek, Jr. (39–48).

1. *Lilium tigrinum*

2. *Oenothera missouriensis*

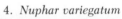

3. *Spiranthes vernalis*

4. *Nuphar variegatum*

66

5. *Habenaria integra*

6. *Asarum virginicum*

7. *Cypripedium passerinum*

8. *Malva neglecta*

9. *Lupinus texensis*

10. *Silene acaulis*

11. *Symplocarpus foetidus*

12. *Darlingtonia californica*

13. *Goodyera pubescens*

14. *Anemone nuttalliana*

15. *Coptis laciniata*

16. *Clintonia uniflora*

17. *Arctostaphylos alpina*

18. *Empetrum nigrum*

19. *Parnassia fimbriata*

20. *Fritillaria pudica*

21. *Cassiope hypnoides*

22. *Callirhoe involucrata*

23. *Cypripedium acaule*

24. *Cornus canadensis*

25. *Phlox divaricata*

26. *Parnassia palustris*

27. *Erythronium albidum*

28. *Anemonella thalictroides*

29. *Hepatica acutiloba*

30. *Caltha palustris*

31. *Aquilegia canadensis*

32. *Lupinus perennis*

33. *Trillium ovatum*

34. *Aquilegia caerulea*

35. *Shortia galacifolia*

36. *Gentiana andrewsi*

37. *Viola pedata*

38. *Iris cristata*

39. *Orchis spectabilis*

40. *Delphinium tricorne*

41. *Podophyllum peltatum*

42. *Dicentra eximia alba*

43. *Sarracenia purpurea*

44. *Amianthium muscatoxicum*

45. *Geranium maculatum*

46. *Actaea pachypoda*

87

47. *Sanguinaria canadensis*

48. *Tiarella cordifolia*

Coreopsis Clan—*Coreópsis*

C. verticilláta

Description: A fairly large group of more or less daisy-like flowers, principally yellow, some of which are already in cultivation but as wild flowers they still appreciate help.
Where They Grow: They grow for the most part in open fields or thin woods, some in damp places, others in dry.
Species: *C. auriculáta*—A hardy, easily-grown perennial from rich deciduous woods and banks, Illinois to Virginia and southward. It likes light shade or sun, is dwarf (18 inches) and a non-spreader. Flowers are 2 inches across and deep golden orange. Reputed to prefer a limestone soil, it also withstands acidity, to pH 5.

C. lanceoláta—Lance-leaved Coreopsis. Erect, perennial, 2 feet tall and bearing 2-inch yellow blooms on long, slender stems (8 to 12 inches) from May through July. Easily-grown, given sunshine and dryish sandy or gravelly soil. Native from Ontario to Virginia, southward; escaped from cultivation elsewhere. Excellent for naturalizing in grasses, along roads.

C. májor—Somewhat similar to preceding but taller (to 3 feet) with larger flowers and leaves cut entirely to the base, making them look like separate leaves. Open woods, clearings, North Carolina to Ohio, south to Georgia and Mississippi.

C. rósea—A slender-branching but short-lived perennial growing from creeping rootstocks in open, sunny, grassy swamps and wet sandy places, Massachusetts to Georgia principally near the coast. The leaves are narrow and grassy. Not a fast spreader by seed. The color is a rose, variable and pleasing. Flowers 1 inch across, July and August.

C. trípteris—Tall Coreopsis. Grows up to 6 to 8 feet but the roots stay in a tight clump. The flowers are small, up to 1½ inches, yellow and anise-scented when bruised. A plant of the meadows, fence rows and open woods, it blooms from July to October.

C. verticilláta—Cultivated in old gardens but now rare. In the wild it grows on dry ridges and in open woods from Maryland to South Carolina and west to Arkansas. The foliage is narrow and fern-like, the flowers yellow and fragrant. Does not self-sow too much. Blooms July to September.

C. drúmmondi—An annual species principally from Texas. Grows 12 to 15 inches tall, the fairly large flowers are fine yellow with a browish center. Compact, flowers all summer. A good species.

C. tinctória—Also an annual. Grows up to 2 to 4 feet tall with two-toned flowers—deep yellow at edge but base and central disc maroon. Attractive and common in cultivation but native from Minnesota and Washington to Texas and Louisiana. Self-sows readily but does not become a pest.

Culture: Perennials from seed sown in fall or spring or division of plants. Annuals from fall or spring-sown seed. Easy.

The Delphiniums—*Delphinium*

Description: A very large group of mostly tall, handsome flowers, characterized by a spur or hollow tube extending back from the base of the upper-most sepal. The other four are formed like petals. The leaves are usually palmately cleft. All parts of the plants are said to be poisonous, if eaten. The species are so numerous we can but touch upon a representative few.

Where They Grow: Over most of the country. For details see below.

Blooming Season: Varied. Again, see below.

Species: *D. andersóni*—Reaches only 2 feet in the sandy and volcanic soils along with shrubs and pines, on the eastern slopes of the Sierras and eastern Oregon and to Utah and Idaho. The flowers, in good heads, are blue and short-spurred; the leaves deeply cut into narrow segments. Late spring.

D. cardinále—Tall (to 7 feet) and scarlet, it brightens the dry, open brushy woods of southern California with its often-branched racemes, May to July. Its basal leaves usually wither by flowering. Deep-rooted.

D. caroliniánum—Grows to 4 feet and has deep blue or purple flowers and projecting wings on the seeds. It blooms in May and June in open woods, sand hills and fields from Ohio to Missouri, Florida and Texas.

D. exaltátum—A tall species, reaching 6 feet, it has numerous wide leaves, 3 to 5-cut into wedges. Its many flowers are blue and white. Found in wooded rocky slopes, Pennsylvania to Ohio, North Carolina and Alabama.

D. géyeri—Of variable height (12 to 100 inches), it is beautiful on the plains of Wyoming, Colorado and Utah, but accused of being especially dangerous to grazing animals. The blue flowers come in dense racemes, in early summer when the much-cut leaves in a tuft near the ground wither.

D. glaúcum—Tall (3 to 7 feet) with stout and woody, large racemes of purple flowers above the 5 to 7-cut leaves, it blooms July to September in moist, high mountain meadows from the Northern Sierras to Alaska and Rockies.

D. lutéum—Much like *D. nudicaule* with purplish-tipped yellowish sepals, it flowers March to May on the open sea bluffs around Bodega Bay, California.

D. nudicaúle—Eight to 30 inches and with gray-green leaves, its dull or orange-red to yellow flowers are not likely to the confused with *D. cardinale*. Blooms March to June on dry slopes and in woods from southern California's Coast Ranges and Sierras into Oregon.

D. tricórne—A small species rarely over 2 feet. Its few leaves are near its base and the few flowers (April to June) are deep blue to purple. At home in woods and rocky slopes, Pennsylvania to Georgia and Minnesota to Oklahoma.

D. vírescens—This one also kicks over the traces by having white or palest blue flowers atop its 5 foot, downy stems. The spare blooms appear in May to July on prairies, Manitoba and North Dakota, south to Louisiana and New Mexico.

Culture: Those listed are perennials and can be grown from seed sown in pots or flats of good, friable but well-draining soil as soon as ripe or wintered in a cool place and planted in early spring. They also lend themselves to division in early spring or after blooming. Transplant to individual peat or conventional pots as needed before setting out permanently. All appear to do well in soils that are only slightly acid.

Description: A group of small, woodland plants, the four most desirable of which are discussed here. Perhaps the easiest way to identify them is by their unique 4-petaled flowers, typical of the mustard family to which they belong. The flowers appear in a small loose cluster well above the leaves which are 2 to 3 in number on the stem and cut into 3 or more leaflets. All grow from a thick and wrinkled root which creeps through the surface layer of humus. It is pleasantly peppery, somewhat like cress, and can be eaten in an emergency but is frowned upon otherwise.

Where They Grow: Rich, damp woods and thickets in moderate shade.

Blooming Season: April and May.

Species: *D. califórnica*—Milkmaids reach a height of 4 to 16 inches. Besides the stem leaves they have basal leaves which vary with the location. The white to pink or lavender flowers come February to May, also according to location. Found in moist, shaded woods in the Sierras and from Baja California to northern Oregon in the Coast Ranges.

D. diphýlla—Two-leaved Toothwort. A small but attractive plant growing 8 to 15 inches tall, producing a modest terminal cluster of about a half dozen white flowers ⅔ inch across and with many yellow stamens. As its name implies, it bears 2 opposite, toothed, 3-parted stem leaves, somewhat resembling those of the blackberry plus basal leaves later.

Generally it blooms in company with the hepaticas, claytonias and bloodroot, seasonwise, and is happy in masses. The root from which it grows is notched and long but continuous, often branched and rather brittle. If it breaks, each piece is capable of producing a plant. It is at home from Nova Scotia to Ontario, to South Carolina and Kentucky, usually in a fairly acid soil (pH 5 to 6).

D. laciniáta—Cut-leaved Toothwort. Closely allied to the above but with leaves that at first glance are radically different. Generally 3 are borne up the stem not far below the flower cluster. Likewise, each is deeply cut as though into fingers and these, in turn, are deeply toothed, while the flowers are often pink or purple-tinted. The root is spindle-shaped.

D. máxima—Large Toothwort. A rare and more or less localized species found occasionally along streams in rich woods from Maine to Michigan and south to West Virginia and Tennessee. It makes a somewhat taller plant than those above, bears 2 to 6 (usually 3) stem leaves which are alternate and have coarsely-toothed but more ovate leaflets. The flowers are similar and white or purplish-tinted. The rootstock is jointed or interrupted and easily broken into several parts.

Culture: The dentarias are all woodland plants, delighting in moderate shade and a rich, slightly damp, humus-filled soil. All are perennials that transplant with comparative ease in the fall and are not hard to grow. They are easily multiplied by the seeds which come in the 1-inch long and narrow pods or by dividing up the roots into as many pieces as seems obvious. This is best done in a coldframe or other protected place and the plants set out into the woodland the following year to help overcome some of the damage done by cutting over our forests.

The Dicentras—*Dicéntra*

D. exímia

Description: Close relatives of the cultivated bleedinghearts, this group rank among the daintiest of our spring wildflowers. The leaves are finely cut, ferny, and the flowers all present variations of the basic bleedingheart pattern. Some grow from perennial rootstocks, others from dainty grain-like tubers and all produce their seeds in capsules shaped more or less like slim peapods.
Where They Grow: See below.
Blooming Season: See below.
Species: *D. canadénsis*—Squirrel corn. This is a dainty plant growing to about the same height as the following and producing leaves which are a little grayer and more finely cut. The flowers are longer, narrower, and lacking the pantaloon-like spurs. It, too, is an easy grower but the mice seem to have a fondness for the tiny tubers which look like small kernels of corn or yellow peas. Like the other, it delights in a rich, neutral, or nearly neutral, humus-filled soil in the somewhat more open woods from the Eastern Provinces of Canada to Minnesota, south to North Carolina, Tennessee, and Missouri.

D. cullária—Dutchman's Breeches. Best known of the group is this little plant of our spring woods. Growing to a height of about 10 inches, it produces gray-green ferny, long-stemmed leaves directly from the ground. The flowering stalk, also springing directly from the soil, generally bears 4 to 10 nodding white flowers, the petals of which are joined to form curious little structures that look like Dutchman's trousers hanging upside down. Blooming time is generally April or May.

They are at home in rich, usually deciduous open woods from Nova Scotia to Washington and Oregon, south to Georgia and Missouri, where the soil has sufficient humus, is a trifle damp and only slightly acid or neutral (pH 6 to 7). In spite of its apparent daintiness it is a hardy, long-lived perennial growing from grain-like tubers grouped together into a scaly bulb.

D. exímia—Wild Bleedingheart. Larger, coarser, and more like the bleedingheart of our gardens but still ferny. It grows to a height of 18 inches to 2 feet, making a bushy clump and bearing nodding, short-spurred flowers of purplish-pink (rarely white). Unlike the two preceding, it does not die down soon after blooming, but, incidentally, also carries on intermittently into September. Found from New York south through the Alleghenies to Georgia and Tennessee.

D. formósa—Western Bleedingheart reaches a height of 8 to 18 inches with long-stalked leaves all at the base and pendant flowers in clusters. The color varies from whitish to rose and the blooming season ranges from March to July. It is found in moist woods from central California north into British Columbia.

D. pauciflóra—Few-flowered Bleedingheart bears from one to three often pinkish flowers with bent-back tips on the outer petals. It is a plant of the high altitudes in the Sierras and mountains of northwestern California.

D. uniflóra—The Steer's Head grows only 2 to 3 inches tall and generally produces only one flower at the tip of each leafless stem. The outer petals are white, pink or lilac and the curved-back tips are much longer than on the above. A native of rocky, gravelly places from the foothills to high altitudes in the Sierras and Cascades of California, Washington's and Oregon's Cascades and east into Wyoming. The blooming season varies from February to June.

Culture: The first four are usually easy to grow and easily naturalized in woodlands. *D. eximia*, however, prefers a more acid (pH 5-6) soil. The first two, tuberous sorts, are best planted 2 to 3 inches deep any time after they die down. Propagation is readily accomplished by breaking up the clusters of tubers and planting out separately or from seed barely covered.

D. eximia and *D. formosa*, because they possess fairly heavy rootstocks, are increased by division, although they can be grown from seed and may even flower the second year. The plants are inclined to spread. Therefore, plant them alone or with strong growers like trilliums.

Not as much is known about the culture of *D. pauciflora* and *D. uniflora* but given their preferred growing conditions, preferably in a rock garden, they can be grown. Propagation by seed is recommended, although division appears to be possible if the plants are strong enough.

Description: A large group of for the most part tall, late summer or fall-blooming perennials with opposite or encircling clusters of leaves and large, flattish heads of white or purplish flowers that look almost hairy from a distance. In all, there are more than 20 species and varieties but not all are worthy of particular notice.

Where They Grow: Low damp grounds along the coast to rather dry upland locations depending upon the species.

Blooming Season: See below.

Species: *E. coelestínum*—Mistflower. A shortish plant, rarely growing above 3 or 4 feet, with blue-violet ageratum-like blooms late in the season and short-stemmed, opposite coarsely-toothed leaves. It is very

E. fistulósum

slow coming up in the spring. Rich soil, New Jersey to Michigan, Kansas and Oklahoma.

E. occidentále—The Western Eupatorium is much shorter, from only a few to 30 inches. It is many-stemmed. The flower heads are compact with nine to 12 white, lavender or crimson flowers per head. Found on stream banks from central Washington into California and east to Utah and Idaho.

E. perfoliátum—Boneset, Thoroughwort. A more tall-growing rather common but desirable species with dull white flowers in large terminal clusters. Its most distinguishing characteristic, however, is the long lance-shaped, yellowish green leaves, grained like leather, and joined in pairs so that the stem actually pierces the leaves.

Like the above, it is a late-bloomer and often inhabits the same wet meadows, roadsides, and waste places, making a pleasing combination with the above. Even its range is roughly similar.

E. purpúreum—Joe-Pye-Weed, Purple Boneset. Perhaps the best known of all the group and certainly a familiar plant to those who have tramped the woods and fields in August and September. Unless conditions are rather unfavorable, it is a tall plant, 5 or 6 feet high, and sometimes may even reach 10 or 12 feet.

The flowers, at the top of stout, little-branched stems, are very small, hairy-appearing and come in large rather solid, flat-topped clusters. Perhaps, the best way to describe the color is a light, grayish purple. They are attractive massed with asters, sunflowers, heleniums or other tall natives, including those above. The leaves are thin, rough, ovate-lanceolate, toothed, 4 to 12 inches long and in whorls of 3 to 6 around the stem.

They appear indifferent to the degree of soil acidity and are generally found in damp meadows, thickets, edges of woods, and roadsides from Canada's Maritime Provinces to Florida, Oklahoma, and Nebraska.

Propagation: Easily grown from seed sown in flats or beds outdoors in fall, division of the roots in spring and from softwood cuttings, if desired.

Evening Primroses—*Oenothéra*

Description:: Golden cups to the sun—or moon—best describes these charming flowers. Some are day-bloomers opening with the sun. Others are nocturnal, opening only at the end of the day. The plants themselves may be annual, biennial, or perennial, either completely unbranched and making extensive clumps of upright shoots or large spreading plants from small bases. Botanically a large and difficult group, it has been cut up into as many as a dozen genera at times. The leaves are usually broadly lance-shaped and the 4-petaled bowl-like flowers are clustered at the top of the plant.

Where They Grow: Sun-loving, dry-land plants, they are found scattered over most of the United States and Canada.

Blooming Season: Summer, frequently July and August.

Species: *O. biénnis*—Common Evening Primrose. As its name implies, it is a biennial or short-live perennial and grows in dry, sandy soils from Labrador to North Dakota and Oklahoma and reportedly in eastern California to British Columbia, south to Florida and Texas, flowering from late June to Autumn. Introduced into Europe even before America was settled.

Growing from 2 to 4 or even 5 feet tall from a large stout taproot, it makes a showy plant for roadsides and waste places as well as fields and meadows. In winter the long slender seed capsules furnish food for birds.

The flowers are night-opening, showy, pure yellow, 1 to 2 inches across, lemon-scented and come in long terminal spikes. The seed capsules are oblong, narrowing toward the top and an inch or more long (and longer than the bracts or upper leaves) while the leaves are lance-shaped, thick, hairy, and alternate.

O. caespitósa—Tufted Evening Primrose, usually a perennial, may sometimes behave as a biennial. It is one of the showiest of all, with white or pinkish fragrant flowers up to 3 inches across. They last only one day each but new ones open every evening. The fruits are short and somewhat winged while the leaves are rather long, narrow, and velvety. Found from South Dakota into Washington and south to Colorado.

O. deltóides—Has an erect stem of 2 to 12 inches with spreading branches and large white to pinkish flowers that open in the evening. It ranges from eastern Oregon to southwest Utah and south into northern Arizona and the deserts of southern California, southward.

O. fruticósa—Sundrops. One of the best-known of the day-flowering species, it is native to the fields and roadsides from Connecticut to Florida and west to Indiana and Oklahoma. Its normal height is 12 to 30 inches, with leafy stems and yellow flowers up to 2 inches across, the outer edges of which are notched. A perennial species, it spreads into clumps.

O. fruticósa fráseri (O. glauca)—Not much different from *O. fruitcosa* but the leaves are smooth, blue-green and wavy-toothed. In the dry mountain woods from Virginia to Kentucky and southward.

O. gréggi—Somewhat shrubby and hairy, the leaves are small and narrow, with the small petals yellow and diamond-shaped. It is usually found on dry, grassy or stony ridges and slopes from Texas to Arizona and north to Kansas, Oklahoma and Colorado.

O. heterántha—The Sun-Cup. Totally unlike *O. hookeri*, below, this plants makes a virtual rosette with its small, yellow flowers nestled in the center. It generally blooms sometime between April and July in meadows and by streams from eastern Washington into Calfiornia's Sierras and eastward into Montana and Colorado.

O. hoókeri—Wide-ranging and variable, this species is usually red-stemmed and 1 to 4 feet high. The yellow flowers may reach up to 3 inches across and grow on a tall spike. It blooms June to September in somewhat moist places through the Sierra foothills and Coast Ranges of California, north into Washington and east to Kansas, Colorado and Idaho. (Plants growing in the high mountains may not exceed a height of 4 inches.)

O. missouriénsis—Flutter-Mills or Missouri Primrose. Depending upon conditions, it varies from stemless to 20 inches in height. The yellow flowers which open from drooping buds are quite broad and appear from May to July or even September on prairies, rocky hillsides and along roads, often on limestone, from Colorado to Illinois and south through Oklahoma to Texas.

O. parviflóra—Northern Evening Primrose. Found from Newfoundland to Ontario, Illinois and Virginia. Similar to *O. biennis* but usually shorter and less branched and with smooth leaves. The bracts are equal to or longer than the pods.

O. speciósa—A white- or pinkish-flowered perennial native from Missouri to Texas, Mexico and the southern Coast Ranges and Sierras of California. The flowers are almost as large as those of *O. caespitosa* and last from sunrise to sunset. Few open at one time, therefore they make no solid mass of color but the leaves do not hide the stems. The fruit is a large 4-winged and ribbed capsule.

Culture: Very simple. They are not fussy about soil acidity and transplant easily almost any season. The perennials can be increased by division and all by seed sown in beds in fall or spring.

Evergreen Shrubs
Kálmia, Lédum, Leucóthoe, Piéris, Empétrum, Cassíope, Phyllódoce

Kalmia latifólia

Description: Four separate genera or groups of evergreen shrubs placed together here because of their superficial similarity and like culture.
Where They Grow: See below.
Blooming Season: See below.
Species: *Kalmia latifólia*—Mountain-Laurel. A stout shrub growing to a height of 20 feet in the South and 10 feet in the North, forming almost impenetrable thickets in some places. In bloom it is truly spectacular with its great mounds of waxy-white or pink blooms against a background of glossy green foliage.

The flowers, themselves, are like 5-sided umbrellas arranged upside down, the 10 stamens further carrying out the illusion by being attached like the ribs of an umbrella. The leaves are alternate, elliptical, smooth-edged, and leathery. Blooming season is May to July, according to location, and the range from New Brunswick to Ontario and south to Florida and Tennessee.

The preferred habitat appears to be slightly moist but hilly places with well-drained, acid, humus-filled soil in sun or light shade. The roots are shallow. Therefore, a mulch of leaves or similar material is needed at all times. In spite of much advice to the contrary, cutting the foliage for greens does not harm the plants provided the roots are not injured and the cutting is done only at intervals of several years. In fact, an occasional severe pruning back to the ground results in bushier, better plants.

K. angustifólia—Sheep-Laurel, Lambkill, or Wicky. A much smaller plant rarely reaching even 3 feet in height it, likewise, blooms later, with the pitcher-plants, calopogons (and arethusas in the North). In general, it likes a similar but wetter soil, growing even on high spots in sphagnum bogs. The leaves are much narrower, a dull green, and the hanging flowers are crimson-pink. Altogether it is not a bad looking little plant. Its foliage is supposedly poisonous to sheep and cattle, but I am inclined to ask why any such animals should be in the kinds of places where it grows to any extent. Surely there must better pastures! It ranges from Newfoundland to Hudson's Bay, south to Michigan and Georgia.

K. polifólia—Pale or Bog-Laurel. A small struggling shrub of about the same size, with two-edged twigs. The leaves are narrowly elliptical, rolled under at the edges and white-green undersides. The flowers are pinkish to lavender, in small terminal clusters, about ½ inch broad and upward-facing like mountain laurel. Its habitat is the peaty soils, bogs, and hillside swamps from Labrador to Alaska, south to Pennsylvania, Michigan, Oregon and California. Among its companions are the Labrador tea, arethusas, and cottongrass with which it blooms (after rhodora but before sheep laurel) as well as pitcher-plants, cranberries, and aronias.

Pieris floribúnda

Ledum groenlándicum—Labrador Tea. Another small evergreen reaching a height of 3, and rarely 4 feet, in the cold, acid swamps and bogs from Newfoundland to British Columbia and Alaska, south to Pennsylvania, Wisconsin, and Washington. The blooming season is May to July. The flowers are small, numerous, creamy-white, and in terminal clusters above the narrowly elliptical leaves. Unlike the smooth laurel leaves, however, the surface is like grained leather, and underneath, between the rolled-over edges, is a rusty wool.

L. glandulósum—Somewhat similar to the above, growing to 6 feet under ideal conditions, found from the Pacific Northwest east into the Rocky Mountains.

L. palústre decúmbens—Native to Alaska and the Old World in Arctic-alpine area. Similar to the first species but much smaller and with branches that recline at the base and then turn up.

/——————/

Leucothoe axillaris (catesbaéi)—Drooping Leucothoe or Fetter-bush, a handsome 3- to 6-foot evergreen shrub from the mountains of Virginia, Georgia, Tennessee and Florida where it grows in slightly moist acid sandy-peat soil. It flowers in April or May with its chestnut-fragrant, waxy bells at the tips of the drooping branches. The leaves are 3 to 6 inches long, shining, leathery, sharp-pointed, and turn a bronzy-red in fall. It is a good shrub for under-planting trees. It doesn't like sunny, windy places and moves better in the early spring than at other seasons.

L. fontanesiána—Virginia to Georgia and Tennessee. Rather similar to the above and is commonly offered in the trade as *L. catesbaei.*

/——————/

Pieris floribúnda—Another handsome leafy evergreen sometimes reaching a height of 6 to 7 feet in slightly moist, peaty acid, well-drained soils. It, too, does best in a light shade and is at home on mountainsides from Virginia to Georgia. The flowers are small, white, and bell-like, appearing in very early spring (April-May). The leaves are fairly large, narrow, and allowed to hang downward. The last two plus the mountain laurel have been collected widely but not wisely and it is now time for us to give *some* thought to their future.

/——————/

Empétrum nígrum—Crowberry. A very hardy, heatherlike, 6-inch evergreen, densely-branched and creeping, its flowers are purplish and inconspicuous. The fruit is round, black and edible, although not particularly tasty. Encircling the globe, it reaches down to the mountaintops of New England and New York, localities in Michigan and Minnesota and the Cascades and Coastal Ranges into California where it grows in bogs and acid, peaty, gritty soils. Like those below, it can also be grown from cuttings of nearly-ripened wood in late summer under glass or mist.

/———/

Cassíope hypnoídes—Also a small, procumbent heatherlike plant of like habitats in the East, Michigan, Minnesota and northward. The flowers, in June and July, are numerous, pendant, white bells standing up on long stalks above the leafy stems. Moisture but good drainage seems even more important than with empetrums. Cassiope leaves tend to be in tiers and the seeds in capsules.

C. mertensiána—A western species growing around the timberline of the Sierras and Cascades from Oregon north to Alaska. Its flowers are also white.

C. stelleriána—This one has white or pink flowers and grows on Mount Rainier and is distinguished by leaves borne singly.

C. tetragóna—Moss Heather is also white, blooms in summer and reaches as far down in the Cascades to northern Washington, It differs in that its leaves are paired and have an evident groove beneath.

/———/

Phyllódoce bréweri—Mountain Heaths, too, are quite similar to cassiopes at first glance but their needle-like leaves grow thickly around the branches and the rosy bells appear more nearly clustered at the tops of the plants. Like cassiopes, the seeds are borne in capsules. Found high in the Sierras under much the same conditions.

P. caerúlea—Circumpolar, reaching only the high mountains in Maine, New Hampshire and Alberta but, like the others, can be grown in suitable rock gardens. It has ascending 6-inch branches and purplish flowers. Blooms June on.

P. empetrifórmis—This one from the high mountains of northern California to Alaska and east in the Rockies to Montana. It also has white to rosy flowers but has shorter corolla lobes.

P. glandulífera—This one has yellowish or greenish-white bells, more closed at the bottom, and inhabits the Cascades and Rockies from Oregon to Alaska. **Culture:** All these shrub-like evergreens want an acid soil (pH 4 to 5) but don't be misled with them or other plants by a casual survey of the predominating rock structure. I recall a number of times seeing such plants growing upon limestone rocks *but* in each case there existed on top of the rocks a thick layer of acid, peaty humus. And they all like a steady supply of moisture, even those which are not bog dwellers. They are shallow rooters and require a permanent mulch to prevent drying out.

The best time to transplant is very early spring just before or as growth is starting and after growth has stopped for the year in early fall. However, if road construction or other operations necessitate moving at any other season to save them, do not hesitate to do so. Just be careful to chop out large balls of soil. If this is impossible, cut the stems back to the ground and set out anyway.

Seeds may be sown in chopped sphagnum (or peatmoss) and sand under panes of glass but this is slow. Transplant whenever they need room and eventually to the wild.

Making cuts half through stems, dusting with hormone powder, and banking the stems with soil over the injuries produces rooted stems which be cut off. This is layering. Air layering with plastic kits now available in some seedstores is also possible with the larger ones.

Softwood cuttings in summer will also root, with a gentle bottom heat, in sand and peatmoss kept slightly damp. For best results dip the cuttings into one of the hormone preparations available to stimulate root growth.

Shortia galacifólia

Description: Closely-related dwarf evergreens, galax and shortia are, in my estimation, our two finest native ground-covers where conditions are to their liking.

Where They Grow: Both are southern plants, galax from open woods of Virginia, Kentucky to Georgia and Alabama both in the mountains and along the coast, and shortia from the Carolina mountains.

Blooming Season: Shortia in early spring at the same time as the daffodils, with galax somewhat later, often well into the summer.

Galax urceolata—Handsome and desirable, it makes sizable mats in acid woods. From a thick mass of scaly, creeping perennial rootstocks with fibrous red roots, it sends up its round or heart-shaped lustrous leathery leaves on long graceful stems. The flowers are small, white, and in spire-like spikes from 1 to 2½ feet tall. Although millions of leaves are picked annually for the florist trade, not half as much harm has resulted as from the building of some roads.

Culture: While sometimes thought difficult to establish, this is not necessarily so. More often it is the result of failure to provide the right conditions—a cool, slightly-moist peaty loam, partial shade, good drainage, sufficient acidity, and a beneficial mulch over the soil. Given such conditions, it can be grown far beyond its normal range, being completely hardy in New England. It likes best to ramble under azaleas and rhododendrons.

Plants may be divided in early spring. Summer cuttings may be rooted in acid peat and sand or vermiculite, or the fine dust-like seeds may be planted when ripe in a coldframe. In any case, carry in pots plunged in a coldframe until ready for permanent quarters.

Shortia galacifólia—Oconee-bells. Evergreen stemless, it grows from creeping rootstocks. Its leaves come directly from the soil and are also rounded but small and lacking some of the firm leathery qualities of the galax. Like galax, the leaves turn reddish in the fall. The flowers are an inch across more or less, upright, bell-like, flaring, and white or pink.

Culture: It too, requires a cool, humusy, acid soil, slightly moist but well-drained, some shade, and a protecting mulch. It is a slower creeper but will also grow well up into New England if given a suitable location. Compared with trailing arbutus, it needs a trifle more shade and moisture to be happy.

Propagation is, I feel, somewhat less easy than with galax. From seeds it is possible but unlikely. Germination is slow and often a failure, and the seedlings temperamental. Division after flowering is past is better, but cuttings taken in early summer are the most successful. Keep them moist in a shaded frame in 3 parts peat and one part sand. Again, carry in pots until ready for their permanent home.

Fairy Lilies—*Zephyránthes atamásco, etc.*

Description: In the fairy or zephyr-lilies, the amaryllis family has given us some very attractive little plants. Low, bulbous herbs, they are fairly hardy and survive outdoors without protection except in the coldest states. They grow to a height of about a foot, producing charming, upright white funnels about 2 inches long. The flowers rise singly on stems from the base of the plant and may or may not be tinged with rose or purple. Generally they are divided into 6 petal-like divisions.

The leaves are bright green, shining, very narrow, channeled, and blunt-pointed. Also they are held more or less upright. The pods are 3-lobed, 3-celled, and contain several to many seeds.

Where They Grow: Generally in damp clearings and rich woods from Florida to Mississippi, north to Virginia.

Blooming Season: Late April to early June.

Other Species: Z. *longifólia*—A short-tubed species with one-inch, bright yellow trumpets somewhat coppery on the outside. West Texas to Arizona and Mexico.

Z. *simpsóni*—Differs from Z. *atamasco* to having a narrower tube and erect rather than spreading lobes. Native to Florida and South Carolina.

Z. *texána*—A Texas species with yellow flowers, tinged with copper and more or less purple-striped on the outside. Flowers 1 inch long. Summer-blooming.

Z. *treátiae*—Like Z. *atamasco* but with nearly cylindrical leaves. Florida to Georgia.

Coopéria drummóndi (Z. brazosénsis)—Rain-lily. Not of the same genus according to some botanists but so closely related to it that it should be mentioned here. It differs from most *Zephyranthes* in that the tube is much longer than the throat. Also, the anthers are borne on short filaments instead of long. The leaves are grass-like, arising from a crocus-like bulb. The flowers are white or rosy-tinted. From the prairies and low limestone hills of southeast Kansas, Oklahoma, and Texas, blooming July to September.

C. pedunculáta (Z. drummóndi)—White flowers are sometimes pink-tinted. Its tube is 2 inches long, flaring into broad lobes tipped with a short point. The leaves may be 2/5 inch wide. Blooms March to July in open woods and fields in Texas and northern Mexico.

Culture: Easily-grown little plants doing well in sun or part shade provided the soil is not too dry. Usually a rich, woods soil, fairly light and well supplied with humus, suits them best. *Zephyranthes* appear to like, or at least tolerate, an acid soil, whereas the *Cooperias* appear more limey-soil plants.

Bulbs of either may be planted in fall or spring, about 2 inches deep and 6 inches apart in irregular groups—most natural distribution is obtained by tossing them, by handfuls into the air and planting where they fall. Both are often found under cultivation outdoors in the South and as pot plants in the North, but they are wild flowers.

Propagation is accomplished by sowing seeds in flats or coldframes as soon as ripe, protected from rodents. For quicker results use offsets or natural division of the bulbs. In any case, they are well worth restoring.

Willow-herbs—*Epilóbium augustifólium* and Relatives

E. latifólium

Description: One of the most beautiful and striking of all the summer wild flowers, producing a tall, graceful, willowy stem 3 to 6 feet high, clothed with neat lance-shaped willow-like leaves. The flowers come in a large terminal spike starting above the topmost leaves and opening upward as the season progresses until fully ⅓ of the total height is given over to the showy blooms and the slender, gracefully-curved seedpods.

The flowers themselves are large, 4-petaled, 1¼ inches across, and a magenta-pink which is quite attractive in its natural surroundings. When the seeds are ripe, the pods split lengthwise and set free a mass of silky down to which the seeds are attached for a free ride on the autumn winds. A hardy perennial it can take care of itself without becoming a pest.

Where They Grow: Usually on newly-cleared land and one of the first to cover the ugly scars of road cuts and forest fires—more than enough to recommend it to any true conservationist. Fortunately, too, its range is most extensive—Greenland to Alaska, to North Carolina, and Arizona.

Blooming Season: July to September, following the sheep laurel.

Other Species: *E. hirsútum* is a European species naturalized in some places along the East Coast. It has slightly-toothed leaves, a hairy stem and smaller, slightly trumpet-like flowers. Also a perennial but not so desirable as the above. There are, likewise, a number of rarer alpine or northern species, including the attractive *E. latifólium* native from Newfoundland and Alaska south to Montana and California's Sierras.

Also attractive high-altitude species are: 6-inch high *E. obcordátum* of California, Oregon and Idaho; 2 to 12-inch *E. alpínum* found throughout western North America.

Culture: Fireweeds are easily grown almost anywhere, including the home flower garden, but culture there is not recommended. Such easy living makes them fat, coarse and lazy—completely losing their grace and much of their will to bloom. It is much better when they must fend for themselves and particularly if the location is on the dry, well-drained side.

Fireweeds are not fussy about soil but appear to do best in one neutral to slightly acid (pH 6-7). Seed gathered in August and September and sown in pots often produces blooming plants the second year. Likewise, this is one of the few plants whose seeds can be scratched into the soil in the wild with any degree of success.

Likewise, it can also be multiplied by separating the parent plants or by root cuttings placed at a 45° angle in sandy loam. These latter methods are of especial value in propagating the rare white-flowered form, because it does not always come true from seed.

H. fimbriáta

Description: A large and interesting group of perennials, some of the better-known of which we shall discuss here. All are upright-growing, producing a spike carrying many strangely and sometimes beautifully-cut flowers. The leaves may be paired and flat on the ground or come up on the stem.

Where They Grow: For the most part they inhabit the bogs, moist woods, or wet meadows, throughout much of the United States and Canada.

Blooming Season: Variable but chiefly July or August.

Species: *H. blephariglóttis*—White Fringed Orchid. In spite of its weighty name, an attractive and desirable species growing usually in highly acid sphagnum bogs only a few inches above the water. The flowers are pure white, fairly large, thickly-clustered on the spike, and have a long fringed lip. In the north it grows quite commonly with *H. fimbriata*, which it follows slightly in season, and along with sheep laurel, pitcher plants, and the last of the arethusas. Farther south it is often found with the yellow fringed orchid, which it precedes a few days. Height 1 to 2 feet, and reportedly to nearly 4 feet. Quebec to Michigan, south to Florida, Mississippi and Texas.

H. ciliáris—Yellow Fringed Orchid. A handsome plant with lance-shaped leaves and large, many-flowered spikes of orange-yellow flowers with long, deeply-fringed lips. Native to peaty bogs and wet, sandy barrens from Massachusetts to Ontario and southward to Florida and Texas. It is one of the more easily-managed species as well as more attractive.

H. dilatáta—A northern species, being found in cedar and tamarack bogs, low meadows, and wet woods throughout Canada to Alaska and as far south as New Jersey, Wisconsin, South Dakota to California and New Mexico. Much less showy than the preceding pair, it is nevertheless interesting with its narrow upstanding leaves and small fragrant while flowers, somewhat similar to those of *H. hyperbórea*. Tolerant of both acid peat and marl.

H. fimbriáta—Large Purple Fringed Orchid. The largest and showiest of the group. Under favorable conditions it has been reported over 4 feet tall, although I have never seen it so myself. The fragrant flowers are a rosy purple, often covering a foot or more on the spike and deeply fringed on the lip. Like its close relative, the smaller purple fringed orchid, it transplants fairly easily and is one of the most reliable of the group. In general, it frequents the moist open woods and wet meadows. Blooms May to June. Considered by some a larger variety (*grandiflóra*) of *H. psycodes* and inhabiting the same range.

H. fláva—Fairly common, from Nova Scotia to Minnesota and south to Missouri and the Gulf, in wet places. Considerably less showy than *H. ciliaris*, the plant grows 10 to 24 inches tall, has a stout stem and bears numerous yellow-green flowers interspersed with leaf-like structures. Somewhat less fussy so long as plenty of moisture and good drainage are present.

H. hyperbórea

H. greénei—Height 8 to 16 inches with fragrant white flowers in a conspicuously dense, conical spike. The two or three broad leaves wither before all the flowers are open. Blooms July to September on cliffs and dryish hills along the coast from middle California to Puget Sound.

H. hyperbórea—Tall Northern Green Orchid. Similar to *H. dilatata.* A northern bog species growing from Iceland to Alaska, south to Pennsylvania, South Dakota to California and New Mexico. The leaves are lance-shaped and erect and the small, greenish-yellow flowers are clustered on the spike along with leaf-like structures. The plant in the photo grew in open sun in wet sawdust into which I sank above my army boots while taking the picture. Flowers June through August, with *H. blephariglottis, psycodes,* and *orbiculata.*

H. intégra—Southern Yellow Orchid. The only fringeless yellow member of the genus in the Southeast. Blooms August to September in Coastal Plain pine barrens, bogs and wet meadows from New Jersey to Florida and Texas as well as the mountains of North Carolina and Tennessee.

H. lácera—Ragged Fringed Orchid. One to 2 feet high and scentless, the flowers are greenish-white and so deeply cut there isn't much left but a skeleton. It blooms in June and July and ranges from Newfoundland to Minnesota, south to Florida and Texas: fairly common in moist upland pastures, meadows and woods.

H. leucopháea—Prairie Fringed Orchid. A stoutly growing species sometimes reaching 4 feet with elliptical leaves up to 8 inches long placed singly on the stem. The fragrant flowers are creamy to greenish, appearing June to August in wet prairies and swamps from Ontario to North Dakota south to New York, Ohio, Nebraska, Kansas and Louisiana.

H. macrophýlla—Long spurred Fringed Orchid. A northern species, taller and larger flowered with longers spurs but narrower leaves than *H. orbiculata.* It grows in moist woods soil in the shelter of firs and spruces with twinflowers, dwarf dogwoods, and blooms the same time as the small purple and white fringed orchids. Newfoundland to Ontario and south to Pennsylvania and Michigan.

H. nívea—Snowy Orchid grows about a foot shorter than *H. leucophaea* and has two or three long, narrow leaves low on the stem. The flowers are white with an upward-pointing spur. Found in meadows, bogs and pine barrens from New Jersey south along the Coastal Plain to Florida and west to Texas.

H. orbiculáta—Large Round-leaved Orchid. One to 2 feet high with greenish-white flowers in a loose cluster. The most prominent characteristic is the 2 large, round leaves, up to 6 inches in diameter, shining above, silvery beneath, lying flat on the ground. The flowers are conspicuously spurred, with spurs whitish, slender, curved, and nearly 2 inches long. Blooms July and August with *H. macrophylla. (Orchis rotundifolia,* often mistaken for it, has one leaf.) Scattered thinly through deep coniferous woods and mossy cedar swamps, Newfoundland to Alaska, south to Oregon, Georgia and Tennessee in the mountains.

H. peramoéna—Purple Fringeless Orchid. It looks like *H. psycodes* except that the lip is merely shallow-toothed rather than fringed. It blooms June to August in meadows, bogs and moist woods from New York to Missouri, south to Georgia, Alabama and Arkansas.

H. psycódes—Small Purple Fringed Orchid. One of the commonest and easiest grown of all the fringed orchids. Similar to *H. fimbriata* but smaller (to 2½ feet), it has smaller, more compact, and less deeply cut, fragrant flowers. By comparison, this orchid is fairly plentiful in wet meadows, along roadside ditches or small streams and in peat bogs. Blooming starts 2 weeks later than with its larger cousin and along with sheep laurel, pitcher plants, white fringed orchids and the last arethusas. Newfoundland and Quebec to Minnesota and south to Georgia, Tennessee and Arkansas.

Culture: Most fringed orchids are not easy to grow. They are natives of bogs and wet places and are usually acid lovers. However, *H. ciliaris, flava, fimbriata,* and *psycodes* transplant fairly easily and are easier to handle and, given growing conditions to their liking, may continue to prosper if protected from slugs, cutworms and snails with poison bait.

So far as I know, no one has yet propagated any of these artificially. Make them as much at home as possible and wait for natural division. The seed is extremely fine and I have personally tried many times to germinate it under natural conditions and in cultures such as are used for cultivated orchids but without success.

Fringed Polygala—*Polýgala paucifólia*

Description: This has always been to me a particularly interesting, as well as dainty, low-growing perennial. It rises only 4 to 6 inches from a horizontal trailing stem, sometimes a foot or more long, just beneath the surface. The leaves are few, oval, evergreen—a bright lustrous green in summer and bronzy-red in winter—as well as clustered near the top of the stem.

The flowers are about an inch long and a rosy magenta (occasionally white) which is really attractive in their native setting. In the center the "petals" are united into a tube which is fringed at the free end, while on either side of it extends a "wing." And it is from this form that arose the highly-descriptive name of "bird-on-wing" by which I knew it in my childhood. However, in addition to these rather showy flowers which are borne, in groups of 1 to 5, in the leaf axils at the top of the stems, there are also numerous cleistogamous or inconspicuous self-fertilizing flowers produced at the bases of the stems.

Where They Grow: Usually they are found in damp, rich soil, definitely acid, from The Gaspe to Manitoba, south to Illinois and through the mountains to Georgia and Tennessee.

Blooming Season: May or June, according to their location.

Culture: To make this plant happy, give it a slightly moist but not wet humus-rich soil in some shade. A rich oak-leaf soil is ideal and a light mulch of oak leaves should be maintained at all times. The optimum soil acidity appears to be pH 5 to 6.

Although transplanting is not easy because of the long almost root-free runners, it would be a serious mistake not to try to save these plants from the path of construction or to neglect having some in every suitable nature trail. Just be sure to take large sods.

While plants can be grown from seed planted in a light sandy-humusy soil as soon as it is ripe, it is not easy to locate the seeds. A surer way is to make cuttings of the new growth in early June, dip them into a rooting hormone, and set into flats of moist sand and acid peat. When sufficiently rooted, in 4 to 6 weeks, pot up several to a small pot, keep slightly moist and under a light shade.

In the absence of a coldframe ribs can be made of stiff wire inserted into a flat and a tent made over them with polyethylene plastic film. With this, one light watering can last months. When well established the following year, the plants can be set out into their new homes.

Other Species: In addition to the above, there are a dozen or more related species. However, as a group, they are not so showy nor as desirable. The flowers are entirely different, most of them resembling, in a rough way, a small head of clover on a slender little plant.

P. lutéa—Yellow Polygala. Typical of this group is this dainty biennial. It grows 6 to 12 inches tall, is upright, bears its oblong to lance-shaped leaves all up and down the stem, and produces its orange-yellow flat-topped cylindrical heads from June to September. Long Island to Pennsylvania and southward along the coast to Louisiana in damp sandy or peaty soil.

The Fritillaries—*Fritilláría*

Description: Whether you call them mission bells, squaw lilies, rice lilies or just plain fritillaries they comprise a fairly large and most interesting group of plants. Growing from small bulbs, many of which are made up of fleshy scales that resemble rice grains, they are for the most part slender plants with unbranched stems bearing at their tops one or more usually pendant, bell-like flowers.
Where They Grow: See below.
Blooming Season: See below.
Culture: Hardy and amenable to culture, they are often divided into two groups. Representative of the first are *F. biflora, liliacea, pluriflora* and *purdyi* which usually prefer sun in open fields and heavier, more loamy, fairly rich soils.

The first group also have bulbs composed of thick, heavy scales on a thin rhizomatous base, stems 4 to 12 inches tall and leafy bases. Some of those in the second group are *F. atropurpurea, lanceolata, parviflora, pudica* and *recurva*. These, usually prefer lighter, well-drained soils in somewhat wooded areas. They usually have bulbs that are low, conical and in one piece, their sides thickly covered with small, round, rice-like affects. Their slender stems may be 1 to 3 feet tall and leafy well above the base.

They are best planted in the fall (late in the East to delay top growth) and 3 to 5 inches deep. In summer do not subject them to heavy or frequent watering but do not let the soil dry out completely. Also, outside of their ranges they usually benefit from a winter mulch.

Propagation may be affected by separating some of the larger scales or the ricey bulblets and growing them in flats or by seeds sown as soon as ripe. Bulbs that multiply by themselves may also be taken advantage of.

Species: *F. atropúrpurea*—Grows 6 to 24 inches high, has broad bell-shaped purplish-brown flowers spotted with yellow or white and grassy leaves borne singly or in circles. It blooms April to July in coniferous woodlands, moist grassy slopes and rocky ridges in California's Sierras and the Cascades of Oregon into North Dakota, Nebraska and New Mexico. Called "rice-root" by the Indians.

F. biflóra—Mission Bells. (6 to 16 inches). Has one to seven, unmottled, dark brown to greenish-purple flowers and a few broader leaves crowded just above the ground, it is at home on grassy slopes and mesas throughout California's Coast Ranges and southward. Blooms come between February and June.

F. brandegei—Tall (16 to 40 inches), its four to 12 drooping flowers vary from greenish-white to pink or purplish and its leaves are often but not always whorled. It blooms April to June under yellow pine, in the foothills of the southern Sierras.

F. camschatcénsis—The Chocolate or Kamchatka Lily usually has two or more browish-purple flowers tinged on the outside with yellow-green on a stiff stem 1 to 2 feet tall. It blooms late spring or summer in moist places near the coast, from Washington north and west to the Aleutians and Japan. Its leaves are whorled and its bulbs ricey.

F. glaúca—Native to the barren slopes of California's Coast Ranges and southern Oregon, this 1 to 3-foot species bears yellow-marked purplish or greenish-yellow marked with purple flowers between April and July. Unlike many, its leaves are comparatively broad as well as near the ground.

F. lanceoláta—Checkerlily. So-named because of its mottled flowers, (purplish mottled with yellow to greenish-yellow with purplish), it grows 1 to 3 feet tall in grass, brush or open woods in the Coast Ranges of southern California to British Columbia and east to Idaho. The leaves (½ to 1 inch wide) are in whorls of three to five on the upper stems. February to May.

F. liliácea—Has white flowers marked with green on 4 to 14 inch stems and narrow to ovate leaves borne near the ground. Bloom February to April in open places near the Coast in mid-California.

F. micrántha—Another tall one (1 to 3 feet) bears up to 20 flowers varying from purplish to greenish-white above its whorled leaves. Blooms April to June in the Sierras.

F. pinetórum— Pine Fritillary bears three to nine erect or nearly erect flowers resembling *F. atropurpurea* on 4 to 14-inch stems above its narrow, whorled leaves that have a whitish bloom. The large basal leaves disappear before blooming, May to July. Found at 6-10,000 feet on granitic slopes in the southern Sierras.

F. pluriflóra—Pink Fritillary or Adobe Lily grows in the foothills of the Sacramento Valley and east of the Cascades in Oregon. Its leaves are clustered near the base. Blooms February to April. Scaly-bulbed.

F. púdica—Yellow Fritillary. Native to dry hillsides, sagebrush and mountains to 9000 feet, Montana to British Columbia south, mostly east of the Cascades into California and south in the Rockies, to New Mexico. One to three drooping flowers are borne on stems rarely over a foot tall. The leaves are narrow and the bulbs ricey.

F. púrdyi—Noted for its greenish-white flowers marked with purple, it occupies ridges in chaparral or pine lands in the northern Coast Ranges of California. It blooms March to June and grows 4 to 16 inches tall.

F. recúrva—From Nevada, across southern Oregon into northern California, this species may be found in dry brush country or woods. The one to nine flowers, which may range through rosy tones to scarlet, are distinctly bell-shaped, with thin curled back tips. The leaves are whorled and the bulbs are made up of several thick scales and many rice-like bulblets. Height 1 to 3 feet. Blooms March to July.

F. striáta—A 10 to 18-inch species with fragrant white flowers, often red-striped, and leaves borne singly on the lower half of the stem. It blooms in March and April in clayey soil in the Sierra foothills of Southern California.

The Gaillardias—*Gaillárdia*

Description: A handsome group of hardy, vigorous plants with large, showy flowers. The leaves are alternate and more or less toothed, while the flowers are large, solitary, and composed of a showy, brown-purple central disc surrounded by red and yellow rays. According to some authorities there are at least a dozen species, both annual and perennial, but all look more or less alike and we shall discuss only a few of the most important ones.

All of those listed below are showy and well worth preserving as a part of our countryside. If no longer there, they should be restocked in public reservations and offer a handsome embellishment for our western roadsides. Perennials, especially, are amenable to picking, if not too severe.

Where They Grow: All are plants of the western plains and like sunlight.

Blooming Season: When happy, most of them bloom a large part of the summer and well into fall.

Species: *G. amblýodon*—A 1 to 2-foot erect annual with oblong leaves, little-toothed and hairy. The flowers are large and showy with their ray flowers entirely red-brown or maroon. A Texan plant not well-known outside its home territory but occasionally found in cultivation.

G. arizónica—A short plant of 4 to 15 inches. The lobed or cleft leaves are all close to the ground with the yellow flowers rising on a leafless stem. Found on plains and mesas from Utah and Nevada to southern Arizona.

G. pulchélla—An erect, hairy, branching annual with ascending branches, 12 to 24 inches tall. The flower heads are 2 or more inches across, generally 2-toned, yellow and rosy brown-purple to almost all brown-purple. From dry sandy prairies of Colorado and New Mexico to Nebraska, Missouri, and Louisiana. A garden escape in the East. June and July.

G. aristáta—A perennial species. Its flower heads are large, sometimes up to 3 or 4 inches across with dark brownish-purple discs and bright yellow ray petals which may be purplish near their bases. Native from Saskatchewan to British Columbia, south to Utah and Colorado.

G. lutéa—In spite of a confusion of names, this is apparently a separate species from that immediately above, differing in having both disc and ray petals of yellow and growing in moist, sandy ground. Found along the Coastal Plain from Florida to Texas and north to Missouri.

G. pinnatífida—A pinwheel-like perennial. It grows about a foot tall and produces its 1-inch broad blooms with yellow ray petals above leaves which are deeply cut and almost fernlike. Colorado to Utah to Mexico.

Culture: All gaillardias thrive best in light, open, well-drained soils exposed to full sunlight and air. Good drainage is essential. In cold, heavy, poorly-drained soils they usually winterkill. In a general way the annual sorts seem to be plants of the somewhat milder regions while the perennials tend to come from regions of heat and drought in summer, cold in winter.

There is nothing difficult about their propagation. Both annuals and perennials are readily raised from seed planted outdoors in the spring. The perennial sorts can also be divided in spring or grown from cuttings.

The Gayfeathers or Blazing Stars—*Liátris*

Description: A large group of perennials generally with tall, unbranched stems from corms or tubers. The leaves are narrow, untoothed, and alternate, with purplish or white disc flowers in heads on long spikes. One distinguishing characteristic is that, unlike nearly all spike flowers, they begin at the top and work progressively down. They also strongly attract butterflies.

Where They Grow: In general, they are plants of the roadsides, open fields and plains.

Blooming Season: Usually summer.

Important Species: *L. aśpera*— Grows 1 to 4 feet and has narrow, rough leaves with some 20 to 40 flowers per head. It grows in dry soil from Ontario to North Dakota south to Florida and Texas. Like all the others, its color is rose to lavender or purple.

L. pycnostáchya

L. pycnostáchya—Kansas or Cattail Gayfeather. Best known of all. It is a tall plant and in August its stalks are thickly set with lavender blossoms in long dense spikes. In this species the flowers are arranged more evenly on the spike than most. Although native to the moister prairies from Indiana to South Dakota and south to Kentucky and Texas, it grows readily elsewhere.

L. scariósa—Button Gayfeather. Another stout handsome species but with its flowers arranged in fewer, larger, and more definite heads, as its common name implies. Although usually lavender, a white form also exists. From dry woods, Pennsylvania to Georgia.

L. spicáta—Spiked Gayfeather. A common species with a closely-set flower spike up to 5 feet tall and with 15 inches of bloom but, unlike the cattail gayfeather, the heads are moderately large and distinct. Native to moist ground, New York and Ontario to Florida and Louisiana.

L. squarrósa—Shorter, it grows only 10 to 30 inches tall and has narrow rigid leaves. The flowers are a bright magenta-purple and in fewer heads than *L. scariosa*. A drier soil plant. Delaware to South Dakota to Florida and Texas.

Culture: The liatrises are very easy to propagate, grow and reintroduce into desirable locations, and supply color along roadsides, grassy woods edges, and thinly wooded or open country. *L. pycnostachya* and *spicata* prefer a little moisture in the soil (most others, a dryish soil) and not very acid.

Fresh seed does not always germinate well but I have had 2 and 3-year-old seed come very well. It can be started in flats or outdoor beds. The first season a few leaves develop above a thickened tap-root. The following year a small spike grows and under favorable conditions may flower.

Dividing and transplanting is best done in early spring. A faster method is to remove the offsets from the corm-like bases. Curtis and Stiles also pulled away basal leaves with heels and rooted them in 3 to 4 weeks.

G. *andréwsi*

Description: A large group of plants found over most of the north temperate world. They have long been considered among the more difficult species to grow. Many years ago they were a special interest of mine and I, too, struggled with them until I was able to grow them in large quantities.

Both perennial and otherwise, they are non-woody plants with opposite leaves and bearing usually blue tubular or bell-like flowers singly or in clusters at the tops ot the stems. The American sorts, as a group, are late summer or fall-blooming, with the flowers giving way to upright, dry capsules containing many fine seeds. **Where They Grow** and **Blooming Season:** See below.

Species: G. *algída*—2 to 8-inch tufts with purple-streaked, greenish-white or yellowish flowers. It blooms June to August in alpine bogs and meadows, Montana to Colorado and Alaska. Propagate by seeds and division.

G. *andréwsi*—Closed or Bottle Gentian. Perhaps the next best known, it grows in rich, moist woodland borders from Quebec to Saskatchewan and south to Arkansas and Georgia. It is shorter (1 to 2 feet high), a long-lived perennial and bears dark blue flowers that look as though they are buds about to open—but never do—in August or early September. It is much less fussy about soil, grows almost anywhere that is damp, comes easier from seed handled the same way and can also be propagated by division of the clumps in early spring or stem cuttings in late spring.

G. *autumnális (G. porphýrio)*—Pine Barren Gentian is a pretty but delicate and little-known species from the sandy pine barrens, New Jersey to South Carolina. Although often found where there is plenty of moisture a few inches below the surface, it will grow in drier places if given a highly acid, peaty, sandy soil. The flowers, often one to a plant, are brilliant blue, 5-pointed upright trumpets, the leaves narrow but thick.

G. *calycósa*—Forms a cluster of 2 to 12-inch stems each tipped by one or three blue or yellow-streaked flowers. Blooms July to October in moist places from the Rockies to the Cascades and Sierras. Seeds or divisions.

G. *criníta*—Fringed Gentian, favorite and perhaps the least reliable of American species. Erect and candelabra-like, it grows from 6 inches to 4 feet tall and bears from 1 to over 100 violet-blue fringed blooms at the very end of the season but I never found it harmed by frost. It ranges from Maine to Manitoba, south to Georgia.

A biennial, it can be raised from seed sown at once on top of a slightly acid loamy soil and pressed down lightly into it. Plunge the pots outdoors in a sheltered place. Soil in which gentians have grown before seems to be preferred because of supposedly beneficial root bacteria. In March take the pots indoors, cover with glass, water from below, and give gentle heat. The seedlings are specks and may damp-off if too wet but must not dry out.

Traditional advice also requires that seedlings be transplanted as soon as they can be handled with forceps. After handling thousands of them, I am convinced no harm comes when transplanting is delayed until they have their third or even their fourth set of leaves. (They form only rosettes close to the ground the first year.) By September they can be transferred from their individual pots to their new home, a moist, sunny, somewhat grassy hillside, wet meadow, brook margin, or hummocks in a swamp. Do this 2 years in succession. Chief pests are slugs and deer.

G. lineáris—Narrow-leaved Gentian. A slender-stemmed plant 1 and occasionally 2 feet high with narrow, lance-shaped leaves and 1 to 5 or more blue (sometimes white) slightly bottlelike flowers in a terminal cluster. Ranging from Ontario and Minnesota southward to Maryland and West Virginia, it frequents the bogs and wet places often at high elevations and in company with some of the blueberry clan. Its culture is not difficult, it is more tolerant of acid soil. Perennial.

G. newbérryi—Its horizontal stems turn up, each tipped with a greenish to white flower. Blooms July to September in moist places at high altitudes in California's Sierras into Oregon. Also propagated by seeds and division.

Although a perennial, there is usually nothing to divide. This leaves seeds as the best method of propagation. As with all gentians, if seed cannot be sown in the fall, keep in a cool or cold place, neither wet nor too dry. Contrary to oft-given advice, I have had gentian seeds safe from rain and snow but exposed to temperatures more than 20 below zero without harm.

G. procéra—A smaller annual edition of the fringed gentian but with narrower leaves and a shorter fringe. Growing from Ontario and New York to North Dakota and Iowa, it blooms August to October in wet meadows, boggy prairies, swamps, usually in limestone country. Seeds only.

G. pubérula (G. puberulénta)—Another perennial with a cluster of funnel-shaped flowers of bright blue generally in October. Like *G. autumnalis*, it has triangularly pointed petals but the points aim upward rather than out. A plant of the dry prairies and fields from western New York to North Dakota, south to Georgia and Kansas, it has long stringy roots and does not transplant easily when mature. Division seems a better method of propagation than seeds. Height 12 to 18 inches.

G. saponária—A bottle gentian in wet places from New York to Minnesota to Florida, West Virginia and Texas. The pale blue flowers (sometimes white) usually come in small groups. Perennial.

G. scéptrum—One or many stems (1 to 4 feet) each with several green-streaked blue flowers. Found in wet places from northern California to British Columbia. Start from seeds.

G. thermális—Four to 6-inch basal-leaved stems with single flowers on longish stalks. Blooms July and August in meadows and bogs circling the globs and south in the mountains to Idaho, Montana, and South Dakota. Use both seeds and divisions.

G. villósa—A greenish-white perennial species with narrow, almost bottle flowers about 1½ inches long late August to October. It grows 10 to 20 inches tall and frequents the shaded woodland borders from southern New Jersey and Pennsylvania south to the Gulf. Propagate by seed.

Grass-of-Parnassus—*Parnássia gláuca (P. caroliniána)*, etc.

Description: Small but interesting and not very well-known plants of the wet places. Never too plentiful, the remaining stands should be increased or, where danger exists, should be established in protected locations.

From a cluster of basal leaves rise slender stems 8 to 20 inches tall and bearing at their summits single creamy-white, 5-petaled anemone-like flowers about 1 to 1½ inches across. The petals are also pointed and delicately green-viewed, while alternating with the petals are 5 golden stamens.

A characteristic and very unusual feature is the single ovate, olive-green leaves which clasp each stem just below the middle, somewhat like shelves. The basal leaves are more numerous, 1 to 2 inches long, ovate to heart-shaped and borne upon their own 2- to 6-inch slender stems direct from the rootstock. In this species the petals are 2 to 3 times the length of the sepals.

Where They Grow: Plants in the swamps, wet cliffs, and moist meadows from New Brunswick to Manitoba, south to Iowa, Illinois, and Virginia, usually in calcareous (limey) soils and rather localized.

Blooming Season: Generally June to September according to location.

Other Species: Less well-known are the following related sorts:

P. asarifólia—Narrower-petaled than *P. glauca*, clawed, oblong or elliptic, and about the same length. Generally the basal leaves are more kidney-shaped, to 3 inches broad, stem-leaves more round. August to October. Prefers highly acid soil. Virginia and West Virginia to Georgia and Alabama.

P. grandifólia—Similar to *P. glauca* but stouter with larger leaves and flowers. Blooms August to September. Found on wet rocks and in meadows, Virginia to Florida and Missouri. Worthy of attention.

P. fimbriáta—Named for the fringes at the base of the petals, this one blooms from July to September in the northern Sierras, through the Cascades, etc. to Alaska and through the Rockies to Montana, Wyoming and Colorado. The smaller *P. kotzébuei* also comes down to Washington, Montana, Nevada and Wyoming.

P. palústris—Here the petals are halfway between the two above in length. Native to the mountains from Alaska, through California and the Rockies. Stem leaf has lobes around stem.

P. parviflóra—From the meadows and wet limely rocks of Newfoundland to British Columbia south to Idaho, Montana and Minnesota. In this species the petals are shorter, only slightly exceeding the sepals in length. July and August.

Culture: Being perennials, they come up year after year and should last for some time, given the right growing conditions. Fundamentally, they like wet locations open to the sun but, given a little shade, they can be made to grow in drier locations. In any case, they seem to like a little lime in the soil, often growing in niches on wet limestone cliffs. They are especially attractive in damp, sunny meadows and should be naturalized.

Propagation may be effected by seeds if they can be obtained—covering the seed pods with small paper or plastic bags helps—sown on moist chopped sphagnum over a light humusy soil in fall or spring.

Division of the clumps is also possible but, be sure to do it after flowering, not before, or the weakened plants will try to bloom and suffer for it. Keep well watered after division and preferably in plunged pots.

Description: Equally at home in the wild garden and the perennial flower border, this attractive plant rises to a height of 2 to 6 feet and produces at its summit an array of yellow to bronze coreopsis-like flowers 1 to 2 inches across. However, a closer inspection will show that they differ in several respects. The "petals" are toothed, more or less, longitudinally fluted, the central discs are more nearly spherical, the individual stems much shorter and the "petals" usually reflexed.

The leaves are alternate, on the thick side, broadly lance-shaped, and shallowly toothed. They are borne upon tall, sparsely-branching, winged stems which rise directly from the hardy, long-lived perennial roots.

Where They Grow: Rich, moist thickets, meadows, and shores. With its species and varieties the genus covers North America from the mouth of the St. Lawrence to British Columbia and California, south to Florida and Texas.

Blooming Season: Generally August to November.

Other Species: While they are of much less importance from out standpoint, a brief mention of related species seems in order.

H. amárum—A small, branching annual densely clothed with narrow leaves. Its flowers are yellow. Roadsides and open ground, Massachusetts to Michigan, to Florida, Texas, now California. Troublesome in fields.

H. arizónicum—A southwestern species with many leaves up to 5 inches long and golden flower heads borne singly on stem tips, making open clumps.

H. bígelovi—A smoothish plant 1 to 3 feet tall, it has two or three stems and few leaves. The yellow heads are few or single on the stems. It blooms June to August in moist meadows and along streams in the foothills, etc. of California's Sierras and Coast Ranges into Oregon.

H. brevifólium—Another golden and brown flowered perennial from the wet pinelands and meadows, Virginia to Florida and Mississippi.

H. hoópesi—This one lacks wings on its 16 to 40-inch stems. The flowers, yellow or orange and narrow-petalled, appear in loose clusters in meadows and on stream banks. Oregon to California, Wyoming and Colorado. It is said to poison sheep.

H. nudiflórum—Perennial to 40 inches with long flower stems and stiffly ascending winged branches. Flowers yellow, sometimes purplish at base. Approximately the same range as *H. autumnale* but not quite so far north.

Culture: Because *Heleniums* have both good looks and a hardy reliable nature, they are excellent to naturalize in open sunny fields and roadsides which are a little moist and will furnish welcome color to the fall landscape. However, care should be taken so they are not planted where they can spread into neighboring hayfields. Given full or nearly full sun and a fairly rich, friable soil with just a little more than the usual moisture, they will thrive and spread for years.

Propagation is very easily effected by sowing the seeds in spring or fall in outdoor beds or flats in a coldframe and transplanting as necessary. Flowering may begin the second year. Still faster is simple division of the clumps in early spring. Such plants will bloom the first year. Propagation from stem cuttings is also possible but not so often used.

H. americána

Description: The two American hepaticas are among our best-known spring wildflowers. They are hardy and long-lived little perennials with 3-lobed, somewhat leathery leaves which require a good imagination to call "heart-shaped." In both species the leaves are evergreen, remaining over winter and until flowering is completed. Then they die down and are replaced by the new growth.

The flowers are shaped somewhat like those of the bloodroot but are smaller, ½ to 1 inch across, vary from purple, through blue and pinkish to white and are borne upon fuzzy 4 to 6-inch stems. Both flowers and leaves rise directly from the fibrous roots.

Where They Grow: Both species cover, more or less, the same range—Nova Scotia to Manitoba, Iowa and Missouri and south to Georgia and northern Florida—generally in dry, rocky, humus-rich woods soil in moderate shade.

Blooming Season: Early spring. They are among the first plants to bloom, usually from March into May, according to their location. The appearance of little round, furry buds nestled down among the old leaves is one of the first signs of real spring.

Species: *H. americána*—This is the Round-lobed Hepatica (formerly known as *H. trilóba*) and perhaps the better-known one, particularly along the coast where its relative is rare or absent. It is usually found in oak or other acid woods and prefers a soil with a pH of 5 to 6 along with anemonellas, fringed polygalas, and occasional lowbush blueberries.

H. acutilóba—The Sharp-lobed Hepatica varies principally from the above in that its leaves are more sharply pointed and it seems to me that the petals are also a little narrower. In any case, even though it is found over very much the same range, the two species are rarely found together because the latter prefers a more neutral soil (pH 6 to 7).

Culture: Generally they are of easy culture, and it is well they are, because they have suffered badly from overpicking, especially near our larger towns and cities, and the woods which shelter them have, to a large extent, been cut down. Supposedly the best time to move them is immediately after blooming, but if taken with large balls of soil they can be moved safely at any time, especially when in danger from man's "improvements."

Propagation may be by division of the clumps soon after blooming or preferably in the fall, but this is slow. Larger quantities are best started from seed which germinates in the fall with the root penetrating about an inch. The seedlings remain over winter with only 2 cotyledons (seed leaves) appearing the first summer. More important, however, is to catch the seeds in a small bag. They are readily lost otherwise.

115

The Hudsonia or Gold-heather—*Hudsónia tomentósa*

Description: A small plant greatly in need of protection from the beach "developer." A spreading, bushy, semi-woody perennial, attractive both in and out of flower, it produces many stout branches that turn upward instead of lying prostrate upon the sand their whole length as do many other such plants. In a very general way it reminds one of heather. It grows to a height of 6 to 8 inches and, at first glance, has no leaves. They have, in fact, been reduced to tiny awl-shaped, scale-like structures set close to the stem and in a rough way resemble the scales of the arbor-vitae. A thick down gives the plant an over-all grayish appearance.

The flowers are small, yellow, stemless or nearly so, and are crowded closely along the upper portions of the branches. They open only in sunshine but, either way, present an attractive appearance in mass coloring. The fruit is a small, ovoid, smooth, one-seeded capsule.

Where They Grow: Strictly a plant of the dunes, dry sandy barrens and sandy shores, it grows from New Brunswick to North Carolina and westward in suitable locations to Indiana, Illinois, North Dakota and Alberta. A variety, *intermedia*, extends to the Mackenzie.

Blooming Season: Varies with the location but generally occurs in May or June.

Other Species: There is another, closely-allied species, *H. ericoides*, or Golden Heather, which has downy but greenish stalks and is found from Newfoundland to North Carolina but is somewhat less well-known. Another, *H. montána*, known to a few botanists, occurs only on the mountain peaks of North Carolina.

Culture: Clothing, as it does, the inhospitable wastes, it is a plant we should give a little help. The few shore reservations at the present time are not enough to save it.

To be frank, it is next to impossible to transplant the hudsonia from doomed wild areas, unless very young specimens can be found, but it can be started from seed. It grows in practically pure sand along with bearberries, beach plums, potentillas, and little else, either in the passing shade of scattered pitch pines or full sun. What makes digging so hard is the fact that there is often much more plant under the sand than over it.

If seeds are tried, they should be sown in equally sterile, acid sand placed in flats and covered with paper or glass. When the seedlings are of sufficient size to handle, they should be transferred to small individual pots or plant bands. In this way the long roots are confined and suffer little loss in the moving. When they become overcrowded and need transplanting again, set them out in the wild, preferably just before a rain without disturbing the roots.

I. setósa canadénsis

Description: Everyone knows what an iris looks like and, for that reason, I feel we can well dispense with an overall description of the clan. Suffice it to say that iris are found throughout the entire Northern Hemisphere. In all, there are more than 170 different species. For our purposes, we shall cover a few native to our part of the world.

Where They Grow: See below.

Blooming Season: See below.

Species: *I. cristáta*—Crested Iris. Best known of all the small irises, it likes barely acid soils and half to full sun. The flowers are light violet with the broad outer divisions or falls crested (3 raised flutings along the center, the middle one orange). It blooms in May. Common on hillsides and along streams, Maryland to Georgia and west to Indiana, Missouri and Arkansas.

I. douglásiana—Douglas Iris has branched stems 6 to 30 inches tall. Pale cream to lavender or deep red-purple flowers appear March to May. In open woods near the coast of southern California into Oregon. Hybridizes readily with other irises.

I. fúlva—Copper Iris and one of the Louisiana group now attracting attention in cultivated iris circles. It grows to 5 feet, blooms April to June bearing usually rust-red flowers but can vary from red and pink to yellowish. The flowers are wide, flaring and have a tendency to droop. Native to the lowlands and swamps along the Gulf Coast, it has been reported north to Missouri and Ohio and under cultivation as far as Michigan and New England. Indifferent to soil acidity but likes humus.

I. innomináta—A small (8 to 14-inch), variable species with narrow leaves from the open coniferous forests of southwest Oregon and adjacent California. The somewhat flatish blooms may be yellow to deep purple.

I. lacústris—Lake Iris. From the gravelly shores of Lake Huron, Superior, and Michigan. It is similar to *I. cristata* but is harder to grow, preferring a sandy, neutral soil with a reliable supply of moisture, has smaller, narrower leaves and retains its foliage better in summer.

I. missouriénsis—Missouri Iris has narrow leaves 8 to 20 inches long and blue flowers. It blooms May to July in meadows and stream banks, North Dakota to Washington, south to California and Kansas—named after the Missouri River.

I. prismática—Slender Blue Flag. Equally attractive but more slender than *I. versicolor*, it grows from 1 to 3 feet tall and bears 2 or 3 narrow, leaves often no more than ¼ inch wide. The flowers, flatter and more flaring, are often a lighter blue and generally are borne singly or in pairs at the tops of the stems. Like the other, it grows from a tuberous, thickened rootstock and bears

I. lacústris

3-angled, oblong seed capsules in season. Blooming is generally in May or June and its habitat mainly brackish swamps and wet places near the coast, from Nova Scotia to Georgia. It prefers a moderately acid soil, spreads more slowly.

I. pseudácorus—Yellow Flag. If you find a yellow wild iris with wide drooping falls it may be this one, a European species escaped from cultivation. Taller than most, it often reaches a height of 4 feet. Widely scattered throughout the U.S.

I. setósa and *I. s. canadénsis (I. hoókeri)*—Another stout species more like *I. versicolor* but somewhat smaller. From the rocky headlands and sea beaches of Newfoundland and Labrador to the lower St. Lawrence and the coast of Maine. In its native habitat it is very variable, from 6 inches on the windswept headlands to 36 inches at sea level. At its best, it bears several flowers well above its 2 foot, 1-inch wide leaves which are always much shorter than the stems. On the flowers, the falls are more round than those of *I. versicolor* and strongly marked with white toward the center.

I. vérna—Vernal Iris. Early-blooming and the smallest of our native species, often attaining a height of only 3 inches and with leaves 6 or 8 inches. The flowers, borne singly, are lavender-blue with yellow centers. It is not common. From wooded hillsides and pine barrens, Pennsylvania to Florida and Mississippi in acid soil. It makes mats but is not so spreading as *I. cristata*, with which it is often confused. Another difference is its erect standards and wide, yellow line down each of the "petals."

I. versícolor—Larger Blue Flag. An erect plant, 2 to 3 feet tall with round, smooth stems, often branched and leaves shorter than the stem and up to 1 inch wide. The flowers are violet-blue and several to a stem. Handsome and reliable, it is found widely in wet meadows, marshes and along ponds and streams where its thick, fleshy horizontal rootstock can roam. It is not fussy about soil, will stand transplanting at almost any time, and appears to do equally well in sun or light shade. Its blooming season is May to July depending upon its location. Newfoundland to Manitoba, south to West Virginia.

I. virgínica—For our purpose we might as well consider this a southern *I. versicolor*, but it is smaller and tends to lie down. Virginia to Florida and Texas.

Culture: All are comparatively easy to grow. What few demands they make are listed above. They can be moved almost any time with care and don't hesitate to move them if a drainage or other activity eliminates their home.

Propagation is easy. All lend themselves to division after flowering. Cut the clumps into as many pieces as possible, allowing a leaf fan and a piece of rootstock (or *rhizome*) with feeding roots to each. Likewise, all can be grown from seeds. Sow in flats in a light, sandy soil. They usually germinate the first spring, bloom the third. Transplant into flats as soon as large enough the first year and protected growing beds the second.

A. dracóntium

Description: The Jack-in-the-pulpits need little introduction. They are hardy, long-lived perennials growing from thick, tuberous or bulbous rootstocks. The leaves are large and are divided into 3 or more parts, while the flowers have the characteristic form responsible for the common name.

Where They Grow: For the most part, they inhabit the rich woods and low grounds over most of the eastern half of the United States, being found usually in some shade.

Blooming Season: Generally May and June, the blooms lasting longer than those of most flowers.

Species: *A triphýllum* is the common Jack-in-the-Pulpit and grows anywhere from 1 to 3 feet tall. Much more common than its companion species, it will grow almost anywhere there is a little moisture, along with some shade, and a not too impossible soil. The root or corm from which it grows is turnip-like and is one of the most stinging, burning-tasting things imaginable. Although the Indians are supposed to have eaten it boiled and roasted, a reasonable boiling with 2 or 3 changes of water still failed to make it palatable. Following the bloom comes a cluster of berries which turn a bright red and fall to the ground when ripe in September. Found west to North Dakota and Texas.

A. dracóntium, the Dragon Root, is much less common and well-known. While it is found from Western New England to Ontario and from Florida to Kansas and Texas, it seems to be more plentiful in the western portion of its range and to prefer a slightly drier soil. Generally it grows rather taller than its better-known cousin and flowers somewhat later. The bloom, too, is different. Instead of a spathe or sheath which arches over into a hood, it remains upright and the long, narrow spadix or "Jack" protrudes far above it into a long pointed tail. The berries, too, are more orange colored and the leaves usually 7 to 11-parted.

Culture: Both species are comparatively easy to grow in most any woodsy soils, although for best results, *A. triphyllum* seems to prefer a soil with a pH of about 5.5 and its relative around 6.5. In either case, seeds squeezed from the pulp and sown immediately in rows ½ to ¾ inches deep in a partially shaded place should bloom by the second spring. However, storing in moist sand in a refrigerator from 6 to 12 weeks at 40 degrees usually gives higher and more rapid germination. Without it, many may not show above the ground the first year. Transplanting is best done in late summer or early fall, although with real care almost any time will do.

C. acáule

Description: The ladyslippers need little description when in bloom. The pink, yellow or white pouch-like sacs which we call the flowers are well-known to everyone and the 2 or more leaves either hug the ground or ascend the stem. (See below.)

Where They Grow: Reasonably common throughout most of the United States and Canada, they grow, with a few exceptions, in acid, humusy soil.

Blooming Season: Generally April through June according to location.

Species: *C. acáule*—Pink Ladyslipper or Moccasin Flower, one of the most beautiful American wild flowers and one of the most temperamental. Yet, with care it can be grown in wild gardens or re-established in woodland situations to its liking. Native from eastern to northwestern Canada, south to North Carolina and Tennessee, it grows in both dry, sandy woodlands under pines, oaks, and birches and on hummocks in deep wet sphagnum bogs. In every case, however, the medium is shy on plant foods, very acid, well-drained and usually at least partially shaded. Also the thickish roots which radiate from the crowns like the tentacles of an octopus do not go more than 3 or 4 inches deep. The attractive pink flowers which generally appear in May or June in northern U.S. rise on leafless stems above the two large oval leaves which lie almost flat on the ground. In the more northern parts of its range a pure white form is also fairly common and similar in every way except color.

C. x andréwsi—This is a little-known, more or less white-flowered, hybrid between *C. calceolus parviflorum* and *C. candidum* which reportedly blooms in late spring in the North Central United States and adjoining Canada.

C. arietínum—Ram's Head Ladyslipper. A small, rare, and unusually-formed species inhabiting the cold, acid swamps and evergreen woods from Quebec to Manitoba and south to New York and Minnesota. It grows to a height of 6 to 12 inches, bears 3 to 4 elliptic leaves and a solitary, nodding, pointed rose-colored sac roughly resembling the head of a ram. It usually blooms a little earlier than the above and is easier to handle if it can be kept cool. Below its normal range it can be grown only in a moraine with a steady underground supply of cold water.

C. calceólus parviflórum—Small Yellow Ladyslipper. A handsome species, not the most difficult to grow in the wild garden, and certainly one which should be restored in public sanctuaries and flower trails. It grows to a height of 10 to 18 inches and bears its fragrant shining yellow blooms May through June. While it is said to be at its best in swampy, boggy situations, I have found it happy on moist, wooded hillsides under mixed conifers and deciduous trees with trout-lilies and false lily-of-the-valley where the soil is neutral to slightly acid.

C. calceólus pubéscens

C. calceólus pubéscens—Large Yellow Ladyslipper. Closely related to the above, even though intermediate forms often obscure the differences. Grows up to 2 feet or more and supposedly in drier situations such as wooded uplands and hillsides. Divides easily and is easier to grow than the small yellow one.

Of the two, the larger variety is more common in the southern part of their range and the smaller-flowered one in the northern. The larger one is also usually characterized by its greenish lateral petals and the smaller one by brownish ones. Together they range from Newfoundland to British Columbia and south in the mountains to Georgia and west to Tennessee, Louisiana and Arizona. Both grow well in woodsy gardens almost anywhere.

C. califórnicum—A native of northern California and southern Oregon, but it can be grown in the East although it may not be long-lived. Unlike those already described, it produces 6 to 12 small, white slippers with yellowish markings on each leafy stalk, 2 feet high in May or June. It prefers moist ground along streams and in boggy places.

C. cándidum—Small White Ladyslipper. Small, white and rare, it grows only 6 to 10 inches tall and unlike most ladyslippers, it requires lime to grow. A pH of about 7.0 is apparently ideal. At home in the marly (limestone) bogs from New York to Minnesota and south to Missouri, it bears its solitary blooms in May and June in full sun or part shade.—It is the only ladyslipper to grow in the open country and increases rapidly when introduced into the proper surroundings.

C. fasciculátum—A small, uncommon and widely-scattered species of both moist and dry, rocky woods from mid-California into southwestern Oregon and northeastward into Canada. It grows 2 to 12 inches tall and bears two leaves midway up its wooly stem. Topping it are one to four greenish or yellowish-white, purple-tinged flowers perched upon curving stalks some time from April to July according to location.

C. guttátum—The Spotted Ladyslipper of Alaska is usually found in open woods and hillsides, often under birches. It, too, has a pair of leaves midway up it 5 to 14-inch stem. The flowers are white, blotched with reddish-purple. Like *C. passerinum*, little is known at present about its culture in the Lower 48 states or elsewhere.

C. montánum—From the oak and pine woods from British Columbia, Washington and Oregon east to Montana and Wyoming and south into northern California comes this plant somewhat like the preceding in appearance except that it is veined with purple. It grows to a height of 15 to 20 inches and bears 1 to 4 showy blooms, in May and June. It multiplies with reasonable rapidity and is amenable to transplanting when necessary. In its native habitat it rests about 2 months—during the dry period—each year and is then best moved or divided.

C. passerínum—From the rich, moist, coniferous forests of primarily central,

121

interior Alaska, its three to four hairy leaves are slightly sticky and borne on the stem. The one to three stems usually each bear one small, fragrant bloom, white marked with purplish or russet spots on the inside.

C. reginae—Showy Ladyslipper. Grows up to 2 feet or more and is considered by many the most attractive. The flowers (1 to 3) are fragrant and white with rosy markings. It seems to like a little less shade than the others and a wet neutral or slightly acid humusy muck in brushy swamps, bogs, and wet woodlands. Generally easier to grow than *C. acaule*, it is not as amenable as the yellow unless given constant moisture from beneath. Blooms June or July. Newfoundland to Ontario and south to Georgia.

Culture: As a group, ladyslippers are not the easiest plants but they are not impossible to restore in wooded areas if attention is paid to their needs. While transplanting is best done in the fall or early spring when the plants are dormant, they can be moved with a large ball of soil even in full bloom if in danger from construction. One way is to cut the bottom out of a large can, such as a 5-gallon oil can, force it into the soil well below the roots, and lift it out soil and all. Then push the soil back out into the new hole undisturbed. In any case, a sizable bed should be prepared.—Soil in a small hole soon takes on the qualities of the surrounding soil.

Propagation is generally by dividing clumps when dormant, leaving at least one bud to each plant, setting the bud just beneath the surface. However, Curtis and Stiles of South Sudbury, Mass., have reported success dividing dormant clumps into pieces with as little as 2 roots and a bit of connecting tissue—no buds—immersing them for 1 hour in a 2 per cent solution of thiourea or thiocarbamide and planting immediately. *C. acaule* went into a light acid pine needle soil; those like *C. reginae* and *parviflorum* into a mixture of ½ peat, ¼ loam and ¼ sand made neutral with lime.

L. *supérbum*

Description: a large group of perennials growing from the thick-scaled bulbs. The leaves are more or less alternate or in whorls about the stem and the 6-petaled, bell-like flowers are produced singly or in large candelabras and may be either upright or hanging.

Species: *L. bolánderi*—A short (to 3½-foot) plant, it produces purple-spotted crimson, mostly outward-facing, blooms and whorled foliage in southwestern Oregon and northwestern California.

L. canadénse—The Canada Lily, most widely-known of the group and a tall, strong grower, it reaches a height of 5 to 10 feet in moist meadows, swamps and damp fields from Nova Scotia to Ontario and south to Alabama and Georgia. The leaves are broadly lance-shaped and are borne in whorls of 4 to 10. The flowers, which may range from 1 to a dozen and a half or more, are yellow to red, spotted, slightly reflexed, and hang like bells from long, arching stems in July or August.

While Canada lilies are usually found in damp places, the bulbs must be high enough to ensure good drainage. The soil should be reasonably fertile, loamy, and only slightly acid with the base of the bulb only 4 or 5 inches beneath the surface in part shade or full sun if the base of the plant is shaded.

Even the bulb from which it grows is interesting. It is made up of a large number of thick scales which look like kernels of corn. Each year the bulb puts out a short creeping rootstock at the end of which is the new bulb.

L. catesbaéi—Southern Red Lily. A little-known but attractive species similar to the wood lily but more difficult to grow, it is a slender plant, reaching a height of about 2 feet from a small bulb with a few fragile scales. The basal leaves are narrow and grasslike and the brick-red, usually solitary, flowers are borne upright at the tops of the stems. Unlike those of their relative, however, the margins of the petals are wavy and the tips long-clawed. Native to moist, highly acid places in the pine barrens from Virginia to Florida and westward to Louisiana.

L. columbiánum—Native to California and the Cascades east into Idaho and Nevada, it grows in prairies, meadows and brushy woods. It may reach 6 feet and bears up to 25 yellow to orange and red, maroon-spotted blooms in June and July.

L. gráyi—Gray's Lily is a small red lily which can be grown farther north. It seldom exceeds 4 feet and bears its 1 to 6 bell-like flowers either horizontally or in a slightly drooping position in July. Native to the open woods at a 5000-foot elevation in the mountains of Virginia, Tennessee and North Carolina, it is little bothered by cold, is satisfied with partial shade and prefers an acid soil. Rhizome-producing, the daughter bulb is found at the end of a horizontal scaleless growth, flowers the following year, and in turn makes another bulb.

L. húmboldti—A tall, striking lily producing maroon-spotted orange-yellow to orange-red Turkscaps in June and July. It prefers dry, open places in the Sierras and mountains of southwestern California.

L. marítimum—As its name implies, it is a coastal species. It is found primarily in north-central California and has dark red-orange flowers spotted with maroon and non-whorled leaves. It grows anywhere up to 6 feet tall.

L. michaúxi (L. caroliniánum)—Carolina Lily. A nodding lily very much like the Turkscap. In fact, they are very difficult to tell apart, but this one is dwarfer, bears fewer flowers, has leaves which are broader above the middle, and its range is distinctly more southern, being found from Virginia and West Virginia south to Florida and Louisiana. Usually it thrives along the edges of pine and oak woods up to about the 4500-foot elevation. Give it a slightly acid loamy soil well supplied with humus in partial or full shade and less water than Canadas.

L. michiganénse—The Michigan Lily is a more western version of the Canada lily found in the wild from Ontario west to Manitoba and south to Tennessee, Kansas and Arkansas. Its habitat, likes and dislikes are approximately the same. The greatest difference, is the shape of the petals, which recurve so their tips touch, imitating Turkscaps. They are mostly red.

L. pardalínum—Leopard Lilies are tall (1 to 7 feet) and bear pendant orange Turkscaps spotted with purple on their lower half May to July. The nine to 15-leaved whorls clothe the stems. It forms large colonies near springs and along streams throughout the mountains from southern Oregon to southern California.

L. párryi—Lemon Lilies obviously bear yellow trumpets with the petals reflexing somewhat at their tips. The leaves are mostly borne singly on the stems. Native in wet places in Arizona and southern California.

L. párvum—The Alpine Lily (2 to 6 feet) may have leaves scattered along the stem. Its flowers are upward-facing and yellow to dark red outside and orange with maroon spots inside. It blooms July to September along streams or in boggy places from the Cascades of southern Oregon through California's Sierras.

L. philadélphicum—The ever-popular northern Wood Lily is a favorite with everyone who has picked highbush blueberries. It blooms when they are ripe and opens its 1 to 3 bright orange-red bells to the sky in partially shaded places. It is more insistent than most lilies upon a strongly acid soil which should also be well-supplied with organic matter. Moisture isn't so necessary, since this lily is native to the dryish woods and thickets from the Atlantic Coast to Ontario and south ot North Carolina. Variety *andinum* listed by some botanists as *L. umbellatum* or *L. montanum* is found west to New Mexico and British Columbia.

L. rúbescens—The Redwood Lily. Found on wooded slopes in the Coast Ranges from southern Oregon to mid-California, it blooms in June or July. A tall lily, it can reach 9 feet and bears three to eight erect or nearly erect white or pale lilac starry trumpets that are often purple-spotted and turn a deep winey color with age. Its upper leaves are whorled but only 3 inches long.

L. supérbum—The Turkscap, one of the best-known of our eastern lilies. Its technical name is derived from the word "superb." A truly spectacular lily, I have seen it as much as 11 feet tall and with dozens of blooms on one stem. However, 3 to 5 or 6 feet is more common.

The Turkscap delights in a fairly rich, loamy soil well supplied with humus and acid in nature. Further, it is easily grown in sun or part shade if its roots can reach a steady supply of moisture while still enjoying good drainage. It blossoms a little later than the Canada lily and is somewhat similar in color and shape except that the flower segments are strongly reflexed. Long-lived, it grows from a large, round, white bulb which is also rhizome-forming. Native from New Hampshire south to Georgia and Alabama.

L. tigrínum—Tiger Lilies may be found as escapes from gardens anywhere in the United States and Canada. They bear pendant, spotted orange flowers and bulblets in the axils of their leaves. Do not plant these near other lilies. Most plants, except those grown from seeds and kept isolated are carriers of the deadly mosaic disease.

L. washingtoniánum—Washington Lilies may reach 7 feet. They bear leaves in whorls of 6 to 12 and up to 20 usually white, fragrant, horizontally-facing blooms in July or August. They are at home in dry woods and chaparral from Oregon's Columbia River south in the Sierras and Coast Ranges of California. One variety turns pink or lavender or even wine-colored as it ages.

Culture: Lilies are easy to move. The best time is the fall so they can become re-established before spring, but in an emergency transplant almost any time. Don't worry about planting depth. It varies with the size and age of the bulb, the soil and location as well as species. Plant large bulbs with their bases no deeper than 5 inches, smaller bulbs less. Lilies can work themselves down to proper depths but cannot push up.

Propagation by natural division is much too slow. For a rapid increase use scales. Lift the bulbs and peel off the outer scales during or just after blooming and sow in a light, sandy soil after dusting with Arasan. Small bulblets should form on each by cold weather. Cover with hay or evergreen branches after the ground is frozen to prevent heaving and leave them to grow until they need transplanting.

Seeds are more difficult. Many plants do not show above ground the first season. Fool them. When the seeds are almost ripe, place them in jars of moist vermiculite at 70°. In 6 to 8 weeks most will have formed tiny bulbs. Lower the temperature to 35° and store until spring. Then plant in flats of light soil. Shade the first year and grow until read to set out.

Lobelias, Red and Blue—*Lobélia*

Description: Moderately tall plants, stout and erect, growing from long-lived perennial roots. The flowers are borne on spikes and are tubular with the upper portion two-lipped and the lower spreading and divided into three parts. Dependable and easy to grow, every effort should be made to restore them, so far as possible, to something approaching their original numbers, for the brilliance and spectacular beauty, as well as the numerous changes in the landscape, has led to their destruction. (There are several other species but the rest are much less showy and endangered than the red ones.)

Where They Grow: Both grow in low, wet soil in meadows, along streams in thickets and marshes. See below.

Blooming Season: July well into September and in rarer instances later.

Species: *L. cardinális*—The brilliant red Cardinal Flower, brightest of all the American wild flowers, grows to a height of about 4 feet with smooth, rarely-branched stems. The leaves are alternate, thin, tooth-edged, oblong to lance-shaped, pointed at both ends and 2 to 6 inches long.

The flowers, brighter than fire-engine red, are made more conspicuous by the five lobes which are held vertically for a full view, the top pair upward and the others downward. The seeds come in a two-celled, many-seeded pod opening at the top. The range of the cardinal flower extends from New Brunswick to Ontario and Minnesota, south to Florida and Texas and west to Colorado and Kansas.—One of the favorite plants of the hummingbird.

L. siphilítica—Large Blue Lobelia (Blue Cardinal-flower) is likewise a tall, erect perennial, reaching about the same height with its stout, leafy, relatively unbranched stem. The leaves are smooth, 2 to 6 inches long and long-pointed, the upper ones being smaller, irregularly-toothed and alternate. The flowers which are normally a blue-violet to faded blue (both this species and the above occasionally produce white-flowered forms) have spreading lobes, too, but not nearly so spreading as the red one. All in all, it makes a fine plant for establishing around the edge of a wet meadow, swampy spot or in moist woodland glades. Its natural range is from Maine to Manitoba, southward to the Dakotas, Colorado, Oklahoma, Texas and Alabama.

Culture: Both are comparatively easy to grow. Neither are fussy about soil although a slightly acid, fairly rich one appears best, especially if coupled with a light or passing shade each day. For either one seed sown in late fall or early spring in outdoor beds seems to do very well. When the seedlings are large enough, space 6 inches apart in prepared beds. They can then be set out into their permanent locations in early fall or the following spring.

Division is possible but slow. A much better method is to take stem cuttings when the plants are in bloom. Placed in moist sand under glass, they root in a few weeks. Rootone or the weakest strength Hormodin also appear effective in inducing more roots and in less time.

The cardinal flower can also be propagated by laying the stems flat on the sand and covering ¼ inch. In three to four weeks nearly every leaf axil, especially on the lower half, will have produced one or more small plants.

The Mallow Groups—*Althaéa, Hibíscus* and *Málva*

H. moscheutos

Description: Mostly good-sized plants, some non-woody and some woody, with broad alternate leaves and large open to bell-like flowers. Although divided into three separate genera, all mallows are closely related and should be discussed together.
Where They Grow: See below.
Blooming Season: See below.
Species: *Althaea officinális*—Marshmallow, a European perennial introduced and well established in both fresh and salt marshes along the East Coast from New England to Virginia and locally to Michigan and Arkansas. It grows 2 to 6 feet tall, bearing long heart-like or 3-lobed down-covered leaves and whitish or rosy flowers 1½ inches across in axillary clusters, June through August. The root is thick, mucilaginous and was once used widely in confectionery. *A. rósea* is the garden hollyhock and occasionally runs wild.

/———/

H. califórnicus—California Mallow grows 3 to 7 feet tall, is hairy with long-stalked leaves and flower stalks joined with the leaf stalks at their bases. The flowers are white to pinkish with crimson centers. Found on moist river banks in the Central Valley of California.

H. coccíneus—A brilliant red hibiscus, 4 to 8 feet tall from the swamps of South Carolina to Florida. This gorgeous species is hardy well north of its native range and needs preservation through culture.

H. lasiocárpus—Recognized by botanists as another perennial growing to 6 feet. The flowers are white or pink with crimson centers. Native to the swamps from Indiana to Oklahoma, Florida and Texas.

H. militáris—Halberd-leavéd Rose-mallow has daggerlike, deeply-cut leaves and flowers of white to pink with purple eyes. Pennsylvania and Minnesota and Nebraska, south to Florida and Texas.

H. moscheútos—Southern Rose Mallow. Considered by some botanists a geographical extension of *H. palustris*. It leaves are narrower, sometimes with three points and flowers up to 8 inches across and more likely creamy. It is found from Maryland to Indiana and south to Alabama and Florida.

H. "oculiróseus"—Crimson-eye Rose-mallow. A color form of *H. maschentos*, the flowers being white with a deep red eye. Likewise a marsh plant, growing from Long Island (N.Y.) through New Jersey and southward. It does not deserve the species name once given it but is an attractive plant.

/———/

Hibiscus palústris—Swamp Rose-mallow. Another tall plant growing 3 to 8 feet high from a perennial root. The leaves are ovate, blunt or rounded, and not covered with down. The flowers, clustered at the top of the plant, are a lively pink and 4 to 7 inches across. It is common in salty marshes from Massachusetts to North Carolina and lake shores inland, as far west as Michigan and Illinois, especially near the Great Lakes in nearly neutral soil. Give it full sun and a reasonably good soil. Slow to come up in spring, it blooms in August and September. Some feel it should be considered a variety of the similar and more southern *H. moscheutos.*

H. triónum—Flower-of-an-Hour is a small plant of 1 to 2 feet in waste places across the United States. Its leaves are deeply three-cleft and sometimes more, sometimes less. The stem may lie flat on the ground and the small (1 inch) flowers are yellow with a dark red or purplish-black eye. A native of Africa.

/———/

Malva moschàta—Musk Mallow. Likewise a European lant, naturalized in fields and along roadsides from Newfoundland and Quebec to British Columbia south to Maryland, Missouri and Nebraska. A low perennial, it grows only 12 to 30 inches tall from a branching root. The leaves are very deeply cut, almost skeletonized. The flowers are 1½ to 2 inches across, pink or white, and somewhat musk-scented. Mostly a June and July bloomer.

Málva parviflóra and *neglecta* are usually referred to as "cheeses" and are rather insignificant compared to the plants above but are, nevertheless, full-fledged members of the clan. They ae widespread over much of this country and Canada.

Culture: All are easily grown not only in wet places but also in much drier ones so long as they are not too dry. The plants are not fussy about soil quality but do best in a fairly good one, preferably nearly neutral. The one point to remember is that hibiscus are very slow to start in the spring.

All are increased readily from seed sown in fall or spring under ordinary garden conditions or by division of the clumps in spring. If the growth is not too sappy, greenwood cuttings can also be rooted in moist sand.

And Some Mallow Relatives—*Callírhoe, Sidálcea* and *Sphaerálcea*

Description: Though members of the mallow family, these three genera are somewhat less well known except in the West where they are at home. The species selected for discussion here are representative of their groups, and possibly, the best-known to most outdoor people and wild flower enthusiasts.

Where They Grow: See below.

Blooming Season: See below.

Species: *C. involucráta*—Primarily a plant of the Great Plains, being found from North Dakota to eastern Wyoming and Colorado to Oklahoma, Texas and New Mexico. It is a low, sprawling plant, rarely over 1 to 2 feet above the ground, growing from a long, thick, trunklike perennial root that often bulges above the ground. The leaves are palmately and deeply cleft, above which appear rose, red-purple or rarely white poppy-like blooms much of the summer.

C. alcoeóides—Less known, a bit shorter and with white or pink flowers. Its lower leaves may be triangular, jagged edged, while the upper ones are cleft into narrow parts. Spring blooming. Native Illinois to Nebraska, Tennessee, Texas and New Mexico.

/———/

Sidalcea hendersóni—On or near the tidal flats from mid-Oregon to British Columbia, this species grows 2 to 5 feet tall and bears dense racemes, up to 8 inches long, or rosey flowers June to August. It also grows from a heavy taproot. The basal leaves are large, scalloped or shallow-lobed, the upper cut into narrow segments. Attractive.

S. neomexicána—This is a vigorous, self-sowing 2 to 3-foot perennial growing from fleshy roots. The lower leaves are round, 2 to 3 inches across and scalloped, the upper cleft into five to nine-lobed parts and the pink or white flowers, which appear late spring into fall, come in a fairly close raceme. At home in the moister soils from Oregon to Wyoming and southern California to Texas.

/———/

Sphaeralcea ambigua—Desert Hollyhock. Although one of most variable plants, most somewhat resemble a hollyhock. It grows up to 40 inches tall and the leaves are three-lobed with scalloped edges. The flowers, up to 3 inches across, are frequently orange-red but can vary greatly. At home on dry rock slopes from Utah and Nevada to California, Arizona and Mexico, blooming March to June.

S. coccinea—Prairie Mallow. A smaller, daintier plant from the plains and mesas, North Dakota and Montana to Texas and Arizona. The stems often decumbent, are 20 inches or less. It blooms June into autumn. The petals are red, about 1 inch across and the grayish leaves about as long.

Culture: What we have outlined for the culture and propagation of The Mallow Group (which see) also applies here. As with all higher plants, they can readily be grown from seed but, being perennials, they can also be propagated by division of the clumps and, if one is of an experimental turn of mind, it might also be well to try softwood stem cuttings.

Mandrake or May Apple—*Podophýllum peltátum*

Description: While not the most beautiful, it is in my estimation one of the most interesting of our wild flowers. When it is happy, it literally clothes the forest floor as far as one can see with its large, paired, round, umbrella-like leaves. When it first comes up in the spring, the leaves are rolled up into a tight fist, remaining closed until the stem has reached the greater part of its 12 to 18-inch total height. Then they unfold slowly like small umbrellas (the stem is fastened in the center) until about a foot across. The flowers, which are like inverted white cups 1 to 2 inches across, then appear part way up on the otherwise naked leaf stems.

Following the flowers come equally interesting, if insipid, greenish yellow fruits that look somewhat like small lemons, and while I cannot say I am particularly thrilled by them, small boys seem to relish them. The taste is somewhat like a poor-quality cantaloupe and is supposedly nourishing if eaten in moderation.

Where They Grow: Native to rich, slightly moist woods, clearings, and partly shaded roadsides, it grows from New England and western Quebec to Minnesota, south to Florida, Louisiana and Texas. It seems to do particularly well in open maple groves. I have been particularly impressed with it in the open-wooded areas of Pennsylvania and Maryland.

Blooming Season: April to June according to location.

Culture: Fortunately, this is one plant that is in no immediate danger of extermination, although continued cutting of the woods could eliminate it. However, it is one which should be found on every nature trail and in every educational wild flower preserve.

Given the right conditions, it is very easy to grow and transplant without much difficulty. After blooming and before it disappears for the season obviously is the best time, but the mandrake does not insist upon it. For best results give it a fairly deep, slightly damp, leafmoldy soil with a pH ranging from 4 to 7. It is only fair to say, however, that this vigorous perennial can crowd out weaker plants.

Propagation: It grows readily from seeds sown outdoors in late fall or early winter. In fact, groups of young seedlings are easily found in May or June where fruits fell to the ground the previous fall.

Since they grow from thick, spreading, creeping rootstocks, they readily lend themselves to division particularly at the end of the growing season. While the fruit is edible, the rootstock is said to be violently purgative.

Mariposa Lilies and Brodiaeas
Calochórtus and *Brodiaéa*

Description: Once again, we are discussing two groups of plants of different families together because their culture is much the same and they are frequently thought of together by wild flower enthusiasts. Both are found in the Far West. Although many are confined to California in the wild and, being accustomed to a dry climate, they can be very exacting in their requirements, most have been grown successfully elsewhere when the native conditions have been imitated. There are three basic types of calochortus: the true mariposas which may grow up to 2 feet tall and have bowl-like flowers; the shorter fairy lanterns with globe flowers; and small star-tulips and "furry" kitten's ears. All are bulbous.

Culture: While they may come from widely differing sites within their area, all should be given a light, porous soil, not too rich and excellent drainage in full sun to partial shade. Plant 3 to 5 inches deep, according to the size of the bulbs, in the fall—after the first soaking rains in the West, late in the East to prevent possible premature growth. In the East also mulch to prevent alternate freezing and thawing. They make ideal subjects for borders and rock gardens but if watering is necessary, do it moderately and where summer rains are the rule lift the bulbs after blooming and store in dry sand to compensate for their usual summer dormant period. Propagation is possible by natural increase or by seeds started, preferably, indoors.

Species: This is but a brief sampling but includes those which appear most amenable to wider culture.

C. *álbus*—Fairy Lanterns or Globe Lilies grow 1 to 3 feet tall and bear pendant pearly white globular flowers April to June in shaded, rocky places in open woods and brush in the western foothills of the Sierras and southern Coast Ranges. Variety *rubéllus* from the Santa Cruz and Santa Lucia Mountains is a handsome pinkish.

C. *amábilis*—Golden Lanterns (8 to 20 inches) are superb with thin pendant yellow globes on stout stems. A native of the open woods and grassy slopes of California's northern Coast Ranges, it blooms April to June. Like the above, it has narrow stem leaves.

C. *catalínae*—From the Santa Barbara coastal area, it blooms with the star tulips, up to a month before many mariposas. Its 1 to 3 foot erect, zigzag stems bear vase-like white flowers set off with a garnet spot at the base of each. It's leaves are linear and about 10 inches long, often with red-brown blotches.

C. *lutéus*—Has 1 to 10 more or less upright golden bowls, often with red-brown blotches, on slender branches stems up to 20 inches tall. Blooming between April and June, in the grasslands and open forests of the Coast Ranges and Sierras.

C. *macrocárpus*—Green-banded Mariposas grow from British Columbia and Montana south into Nevada and California, supposedly doing best in decomposed pumice. The flowers are large upright bells, blue-lilac striped with green, and may reach a height of 20 inches. The bulb is also large and the stout stem has few leaves.

C. *monophýllus*—Sierra Star Tulip (3 to 8 inches) has yellow flowers, densely bearded and often marked with a brown spot. Native to open pine forests, in the foothills east of the Sacramento Valley, it blooms in April and May and tolerates more water than the large mariposas.

C. spléndens—The Lilac Mariposa grows 8 to 24 inches tall, has 6-inch basal leaves and upward facing bells of pinky-lilac, frequently with purple spots. At home on dry slopes in grasslands, chaparrel and pine woods, it inhabits the Coast Ranges of California. May and June.

C. tólmiei—Pussy Ears. A small species (4 to 16 inches), it has purplish-tinged, erect white or creamy petals, densely hairy inside, and remains in bloom a long time. It is found in dry woods and rocky places in the Coastal Ranges from Washington south to mid-California.

C. venústus—Butterfly Tulips may reach 24 inches. Flower color varies— white, yellow, dark red, purple, each petal with one or two reddish blotches. At home in sandy grass and pinelands, it is found in the southern Coast Ranges and Sierras. It is one of the easier species to grow. Blooms May to July.

C. uniflórus—The Meadow Tulip prefers moist places and offsets freely. It is a very low-growing sort (4 to 10 inches), its clear lilac flowers not much above the ground, are over-topped by the leaves. Native from southern Oregon south through the Coast Ranges, it responds to good treatment.

/———/

Description: Although many are extremely variable, for the most part brodiaeas can also be divided into three groups: (1) those with tight clusters of quite small, vase-like flowers; (2) more open clusters of star-like flowers; (3) widely spaced umbels of more lily-like blooms. All bear their flowers at the tops of the stems and when the clusters are large, they usually open over an extended period.

Species: *B. capitáta*—Blue Dicks, belong to the first group and the flower heads resemble those of chives. It grows 6 to 24 inches tall, has long grasslike leaves, is long-cormed and is early blooming. Native from Oregon to Baja, California, Utah and New Mexico. Give it a loose, perfectly-drained loamy soil with a little humus. (Sometimes listed as *Dichelostémma*).

B. coronária—Harvest Brodiaea grows only 1 foot tall and has loose clusters of lilac bells. It blooms May to July, sometimes blanketing the landscape in dry soils on grassy wooded slopes and even alkaline plains in the Coastal Mountains and Sierras from Vancouver through California.

B. hyacinthína—Wild Hyacinths belong to the group with flattened corms, resembling crocus. The leaves are grasslike and the 10 to 30 fairly large, white to purplish flowers are borne in good-sized umbels. The height, 1 to 2 feet. Prefers lower, somewhat moister ground than most and is easier to grow. Native from British Columbia to Idaho, Nevada and southern California. (also listed as a *Tritéleia*).

B. ixioídes—Golden Brodiaea belongs in the same group as *B. hyacinthína* but the flowers are usually yellow and its height from 3 to 24 inches. Found from Oregon to southern California.

B. láxa—Triplet Lily is another in this same (*Triteleia*) group. Showy and one of the best, its white to blue flowers are borne April to August also on stems up to 2 feet, in the Sierras and Coast Ranges of California into Oregon.

B. mínor—Small (to 12 inches), it has a corm that is not flattened and bearing many strong offsets. The flower cluster may be loose and spreading and the blooms violet and star-like. California to Oregon. May and June bloom.

B. multiflóra—Another "*Dichelostemma*" with flowers in small, almost spherical, clusters, blue to violet and 1 to 3 feet high. Blooms May and June on open and wooded slopes in California and Oregon to Utah.

B. penduncularis—The Long-Rayed Brodiaea grows to 3 feet and the small, white or lilac-tinged flowers have very long stalks making them look like 4th of July sparklers. They flower May to July in moist places in California's northern Coast Ranges. Rare. A *Triteleia* type and very cormiferous.

B. pulchélla—Another with small, tight flower heads, usually purple. It grows 1 to 2 feet tall, blooms March to May on hills and plains through California, into Oregon, Utah and Arizona. Like the other *"Dichelostemmas,"* it may be planted among drought-tolerant shrubs, mints, lupines, or penstamons in dry climates.

B. stelláris—Like *B. minor* this one prefers heavier soil and comparatively moist situations. The three to six white-centered, purple flowers are fairly large, starry and long-lasting. Growing to 16 inches high, they flower May to July in California's northern Coast Ranges.

Marsh Marigolds—*Cáltha palústris* and Its Relatives

Description: A stocky, hollow-stemmed plant with buttercup-like flowers of a deep, rich, bright golden yellow rising from high up on the stems which bear the thickish, round to kidney-shaped leaves. Unfortunately, this thickness brings with it a succulence which has caused its undoing. The plant has been much sought for spring greens, being cooked and eaten like spinach. The normal height is 1 to 2 feet. A double form also exists and is occasionally offered for sale by dealers.

Where They Grow: Common in swamps, fresh water marshes, or along streams across Canada to the Carolinas, Tennessee, North Dakota and Nebraska.

Blooming Season: April or May in the latitude of New York.

Other Species: *C. asarifólia*—Gingerleaved Marigold has single yellow flowers in July or August. Its stems may lie on the ground and bear short-stalked leaves besides the blossoms. Bogs near the coast, Oregon to Alaska.

C. biflóra—Broadleaved Marsh Marigold has leaves as wide or wider than long, up to 6 inches, and usually two white flowers per stem, as the snow recedes. Oregon to Alaska at high elevations in the southern parts.

C. hówelli—Has leaves much like *C. biflora* but no bract on the stem bearing the single white flower. Found in marshy spots in the Sierras and Coast Ranges of California and Oregon, blooming May to July.

C. leptosépala—Mountain Marigold. Its leaves are ovate, round-toothed and up to 2¾ inches. Flower stalks usually bear solitary basal leaves and one or two white flowers, May to August. At high altitudes from Utah and Colorado to Montana, Oregon and Alaska.

Culture: While the marsh marigold is often found in several inches of water, this is not necessary. Given a heavy, mucky soil and a plentiful supply of moisture, it will grow even in most gardens. It is not too fussy about soil acidity. A reaction of pH 5 to 7 will satisfy it, so long as it does not dry out. In winter simply turn an empty berry basket over it to protect the crown from the sun and drying winds.

Like most spring wild flowers, it likes full sun before the leaves come out on the trees and shade after. By midsummer the plant has usually died down, leaving scarcely a trace.

Propagation is very simple. The plants may be lifted gently out of the soft mud, the long, coarse roots washed free of soil, and the crown separated carefully after the flowering season is over. One fair-sized clump may yield as many as 8 to 10 strong divisions. Replanted, they can be left undisturbed for many years or subdivided periodically.

Seed planted while it is still fresh and kept constantly wet—as in a pot or flat plunged near a brook—will usually germinate the first spring and produce flowering-sized plants by the third year.

Meadow-beauty or Deergrass—*Rhéxia virgínica*

Description: An interesting and attractive but not well-known little plant for the moist acid places. It attains a height of 10 to 24 inches, has square stems and grows from perennial, usually tuberous roots. The leaves are light green, ovate, pointed at either end, 1 to 2 inches long, and come in pairs up the stem.

The flowers are 1 to 1½ inches across, a deep magenta pink and are characterized by only 4 broad petals, instead of the more commonly seen 5 or 6, with large golden anthers. Likewise, the petals often fall by early afternoon.

After the flowers are gone, they are followed by a four-valved capsule bearing numerous rough, curved seeds.

Where They Grow: Generally found in more or less wet open woods and edges of bogs and swamps in acid peat, sand or gravel from Nova Scotia to Ontario, south to Florida and Louisiana.

Blooming Season: July to September, according to location.

Other Species: For practical purposes only the one above need be discussed. However, a few other closely-related and for the most part similar species have been set apart: *R. ciliósa* from the damp pine barrens, Maryland to Florida and Louisiana; *R. aristósa*, wet pine barrens, New Jersey to Georgia; *R. mariána*, Massachusetts to Kentucky and Florida, west to Missouri and Texas; *R. intérior*, an inland species from Missouri, Kansas, Oklahoma and Arkansas; and *R. ventricósa*, found in both wet and dry soils from Virginia to North Carolina.

Culture: Given the proper conditions of a continuous supply of moisture available to its roots, a very acid (pH 4 to 5) sandy or peaty soil and no more than a light shade, it will do rather well. It is a fine plant for naturalizing around the edges of ponds, lakes, or swamps and bogs, where its color will be a welcome sight to morning trampers, especially during the summer when color is not so plentiful as later. Whether the name "deergrass" has any bearing upon the habits of those animals, I do not know. It will also grow in fairly dry rock gardens if the soil is sufficiently acid. In any case, plant in sufficient quantities to make a suitable showing.

Propagation: Easily grown from seed sown in flats as soon as ripe in any peaty or sand acid soil. Seedlings will appear in the srping and the plants will flower their second year. This is also one of the few plants that can be established by scattering seeds directly in the wild in suitable locations. However, if sowing is delayed until late spring, the seed may lie dormant a whole year.

Stem cuttings made in early summer also root easily in sand in about 3 or 4 weeks and make good tubers the same season. When setting out, be careful to avoid locations where there are extreme rises and falls of water level. These are fatal to *Rhexias*.

"Meat-eating" Plant—*Sarracénia, Darlingtónia,* etc.

S. *purpúrea*

Description: Perennial plants whose leaves are shaped like pitchers, tubes or trumpets, the inner surface of which exudes a juice with the power of digesting insects which drown in the mixture of rainwater and this fluid. The tubes usually are lined with downward pointing hairs, as well, to make escape of the insects impossible. The flowers rise singly from the crown and are composed of 5 sepals, 5 petals, and a curious "inverted-umbrella" structure on the underside. The seeds are borne in great numbers.

Where They Grow: All are natives of the swamps, bogs, or wet places of the New World—and nearly all eastern.

Blooming Season: Late spring or summer according to species and location.

Species: S. *cátesbaei*—Catesby's Pitcher-plant. A clear-cut hybrid between S. *purpurea* and S. *flava*, a striking plant with the narrow trumpets of S. *flava* but the prominent wings and some of the purplish markings of the purple parent. The flower, too, is a combination of pinkish and greenish. Apparently, it can propagate itself like a species. Virginia to Florida.

S. *fláva*—Yellow Pitcher-plant. A species common along the southern coastal plain, where its 3-foot narrow green pipe-organ trumpets and yellow blooms dot the wet pinelands and bogs. It ranges from Virginia to Florida and blooms in April or May. It is hardy and apparently the best of the southern species for growing in the North.

S. *leucophýlla (S. drúmmondi)*—Tall Purple-trumpet. Leaves tall and narrow like S. *flava* but white at the top with showy green and purple veining. The flowers are of a more intense purple-red than other species. Likewise a coastal plain species, it is found from Georgia to Florida and Mississippi, in wet places. Because of its habitat, it suffers not so much from flower-picking as from swamp drainage, road building, and other operations.

S. *mínor*—The Hooded Pitcher-plant differs from the more common species in that the lid of the pitcher bends over to form a cover for the long, narrow tube instead of standing erect. Its flowers are yellow and the leaves reach a height of about 2 feet on the coastal plain from southern North Carolina to Northern Florida. An interesting species and, like the others, a plant well worth preserving for future generations.

S. *oreophíla*—Has several short, flat leaves in addition to erect trumpets and small, greenish-yellow petals. Found in the Georgia and Alabama mountains.

S. *psittácina*—Parrot Pitcher-plant produces numerous small, curved pitchers often not over 6 inches long. They are hooded but not "lidded." Rather, they curve over in cobra-like fashion and are usually marked with red or purple. The flowers vary from purple to greenish with the petals often rolled to appear narrower than on the other reddish sorts. Moist pine lands, even under water.

136

Georgia and North Florida to Louisiana.

S. purpúrea—Common Pitcher-plant. The most widespread of the species, being found from Labrador to the Mackenzie, south to Florida and Louisiana. So common is it in the North that it was the National and is now the Provincial Flower of Newfoundland where it carpets the bogs for miles. Usually it is found growing in full sun in live sphagnum with the roots only occasionally reaching into muck or other soil.

For companions it chooses cranberries, Labrador tea, *Kalmia polifolia*, sheep-laurel, aronias, alders, sundews, and various orchids. Its blooming season is late May well into July, after rhodora and along with arethusa, Labrador tea, and aronias. Its identifying characteristics are the broad pitcher or powder horn-like leaves, often purple-toned, and the red-purple flowes. Height 1 foot. Drainage and collectors are its worst enemies.

S. rúbra—Sweet Pitcher-plant. A fragrant species found along the coastal plain from North Carolina to West Florida. The pitchers are erect, hooded but shorter and more open than *S. minor*, reaching a height of 20 inches. The flowers are crimson to purplish-red and green, and rise well above the red-veined pitchers.

Darlingtónia (Chrysámphora) califórnica—Cobra Plant. This is a close relative of the pitcher-plants with tall, purplish-shaded pitchers that grow up to 30 inches high and curve over like the head of a cobra so the opening points down. Further, they have an appendage attached near the opening which looks like the snake's forked tongue. Its purple-red flowers are similar to those of the *Sarracenias* except that the sepals are narrower and the "umbrella" structure is much reduced.

Like the others, it is a bog dweller. Although it confines itself to northern California, southern Oregon, and the Seattle area, and is the only pitcher-producing plant in the Far West, it has grown in New England when given winter protection. Unfortunately, because of its unusual form, it is exploited well beyond its rate of reproduction and needs assistance.

Culture: Given the proper acid bogs or swampy conditions under which they are found in nature, pitcher-plants are not difficult to grow. However, care must be exercised to keep the crowns at the surface, well above the normal water level, with only the roots reaching down. Nor do the roots need to find a rich soil for sustenance. In Newfoundland, for instance, I have seen miles of the northern species growing in nothing but sphagnum as far down as one would care to dig. But, most species do seem to prefer full, or at least a generous amount of sun.

They are easily increased by division of the crowns at almost any season and by seeds sown in flats of peat to which a little sand and loam has been added. A half-inch topping of shredded sphagnum also helps and the flats must be kept from drying out. Flowering normally takes 3 to 5 years.

Note: There are also other "insect-eating" plants such as the Venus fly-trap, (*Diónaea*) from the Carolinas and several sundews (*Drósera*) which space does not allow us to cover. However, habitats and cultural requirements are much like those of the plants above.

Three Bog Orchids—*Arethúsa, Calýpso* and *Calopógon*

Arethúsa bulbósa

Description: See below.
Where They Grow: See below.
Blooming Season: May in southern portions to July in Newfoundland and similar areas.
Species: Since these 3 species are all orchids, bloom at approximately the same time, and are generally associated in the public mind, we shall here consider them altogether.

Arethúsa bulbósa—Once fairly common in acid peat bogs and wet meadows from Newfoundland (where the accompanying photo was taken) to the Carolinas and west to Ontario, Indiana, and Wisconsin, it is now fast disappearing. One of our most graceful orchids, it makes a plant 6 to 10 inches high and bears, usually a single dainty light rose-colored bloom best described by the photo above. The lone, narrow leaf is almost grasslike and appears after the flowers are past. Both grow from a small, ovoid bulb about ½ inch in diameter. One of the dangers in picking the flower is that the bulb is only lightly anchored in the loose sphagnum and is easily pulled out. Blooms May to August.

/————/

Calýpso bulbósa—Even more widely spread than the preceding, it is native to northern Europe, Asia, and across Canada south to New England, Minnesota, California and in the mountains as far as Arizona. It, too, grows from a bulb-like structure and bears but one leaf and one flower, but the bloom, instead of having a broad, flat lip is more sack-shaped and the leaf is about 2 inches long, broadly triangular and appears with the flowers. It stands shade and is usually found in cool, mossy woods (in limestone areas) particularly around arbor-vitae.

/————/

Calopógon tuberósus (C. pulchéllus)—The Grass Pink is easily distinguished from the others. It is taller, growing up to 18 inches, has a graceful, more willowy stem bearing 3 to 7 pinkish-magenta blooms which are about 1 inch broad, more wheel-shaped than the others and possess delightful raspberry scent. The leaf is narrow and grasslike but, unlike the arethusa, appears with the bloom. It, too, is bulb-forming and is found from Newfoundland to Ontario and Minnesota, but continues south to Florida and Texas in sphagnum bogs and wet meadows or savannas.

C. pállidus—A smaller plant with paler flowers inhabiting wet places from Virginia to Florida and Louisiana.

Cultures: All transplant at almost any season but *do not survive under cultivation.* Move them *only if faced with certain destruction* and then place them only under conditions exactly like those from which they came. Propagation is best left to natural increase. Seed is minute and, so far as I know, has never been germinated artificially. Protect from slugs and rodents.

Some Other Orchids—*Pogónia* Group, *Spiránthes, Goodyéra*

Description:
Where They Grow: See below.
Blooming Season:

Species: Not closely related nor similar in looks, these three groups are considered together purely for convenience. The old genus Pogonia has in turn now been divided up into *Cleístes, Isótria, Pogónia,* and *Triphóra.*

C. divaricáta—Grows 12 to 18 inches, bearing single pinkish blooms at the tops of the stems. Single lance-shaped leaves are borne halfway up on addition to basal ones. Blooms June, early July, in acid meadows or damp pine barrens, New Jersey to Florida and Kentucky to Texas.

/————/

I. medeoloídes—Lesser Five-Leaved Pogonia. Rare. Greenish-yellow flowers (April and May) and leaves in 5's encircling the stem. Eight to 9 inches. Dry woods, Vermont south to Pennsylvania and North Carolina and west to Missouri.

I. verticilláta—Whorled Pogonia. A dull purplish and greenish-yellow flower with a long stem, long, narrow, erect, and a circle of 5 leaves resembling those of the Indian cucumber. Height 6 to 12 inches. Blooming season, April to June. Acid woods, New England to Wisconsin, south to Florida and Texas. Like the rose pogonia, runners form colonies.

/————/

P. ophioglossoídes—Rose Pogonia or Bog Rose is slender (6 to 12 inches) with solitary, nodding, raspberry-scented, rosy blooms resembling a not-fully-opened arethusa. Usually there is a tiny leaf just below the blossom and a larger, broadly lance-shaped one halfway up the stem. An inhabitant of swamps, bogs, and wet meadows, often in company with the calopogon. Newfoundland to Ontario, south to Minnesota, Tennessee, Florida and Texas. Blooming season: June to August.

/————/

T. trianthóphora—Three-birds. Orchid. If any pogonia could be called manageable, this would be it, but it often goes dormant for years. Tuberoid, it grows in loamy woods soils under a wide variety of conditions from Maine to Wisconsin and Missouri, southward to Florida and Texas. Less showy than the rose pogonia, it grows 3 to 8 inches and bears three but smaller, pink or white pendulous flowers August to September. Also spreads by runners.

Culture: Pogonias are difficult. Do not attempt any unless conditions are ideal or necessity requires it. I once grew rose pogonias for years in a metal tray full of sphagnum constantly wet from below but, even there, they eventually gave up the ghost. When happy, rose pogonias spread into clumps by runners.

/————/

Spiranthes cérnua—Ladies' Tresses are marsh orchids with 1 to 2-foot, narrow twisted flower spikes and flowers that are small, fragrant, outward facing creamy tubes. Stem leaves, too, are narrow and stay close to the stems. Spiranthes are not hard to transplant and can thrive in wet open meadows, often surviving land clearing. Indifferent to soil acidity and reasonably common from Quebec to South Dakota, Florida and Texas. Blooms late August-September.

S. gracílis—Slender Ladies' Tresses. Probably the easiest grown but less showy. The stem is slender and the flowers smaller, earlier, and more spirally arranged. It grows in drier slightly acid grasslands and open woods from Nova

Scotia to Manitoba south to Florida and Texas. It is best moved in the winter rosette stage and can be flowered from seed in 3 years.

S. *gráyi*—Little Pearl-Twist is a smallish (to 2 feet), slender plant with narrow leaves on short stalks. The flowers are small, white and in close spirals or, sometimes, all on one side. It blooms March to October according to location. Found Massachusetts to Michigan and south to Arkansas, Texas and Florida.

S. *laciniáta*—Lace-Lip Orchid. Characterized by narrow, sheathing leaves on the lower parts of the stems and closely-spiralled white flowers with narrow, toothed lips. It blooms May to August and is found in bogs, marshes and shallow water from New Jersey to Florida and west to Texas. It is thought, by some botanists, to be a natural hybrid.

S. *parasítica*—This one has small, pink flowers with green-striped-white lips all on one side of the stem. The leaves are all at the base and often missing at flowering time, giving rise to the mistaken idea it is parasitic. From West Texas into Arizona and Mexico, blooming early in the summer.

S. *romanzoffiána*—Hooded Ladies' Tresses are not fussy about soil so long as it is sterile. Native to bogs, moist grassy places, and gravelly shores, Labrador to Alaska south to New York, Iowa, Utah, southern California and New Mexico. Propagated by seed and sometimes division. Other species also exist but the differences are not sufficient to warrant discussion.

S. *vernális*—Narrow-Leaved Ladies Tresses. One of the tallest species (96 to 44 inches), it often has grassy leaves on the stem as well as at the base, while the flowers are fragrant but often yellowish instead of a clean white. A native of wet meadows, bogs, pinelands and woods from Quebec to Nebraska and south to Florida and New Mexico.

/————/

G. *oblongifólia*—Typical of a group of small, interesting but not showy orchids. The leaves are the most interesting part, forming a rosette near the ground, they are dark green with a network of white. The flowers are white or greenish and borne spiralling loosely or on one side of a slender spike that may reach up to 18 inches. They grow in the leafmold on the forest floor. Transplanting is easy. Summer blooming, they are found from Nova Scotia to Alaska, south to Maine, Wisconsin, Wyoming, California and New Mexico.

G. *pubéscens*—Downy Rattlesnake Plantain. Similar but with slightly smaller leaves. The flowers encircle the stem making a dense cylindrical spike. Grows Newfoundland to Minnesota and south to Arkansas and Georgia. They are frequently used over winter to add interest to terrariums. When so used they should be planted back outside in the spring.

G. *répens*—Creeping Rattlesnake Plantain grows to about 14 inches, has still smaller leaves (2 inches), dark (or white-bordered) instead of white veins, slender runners and flowers sometimes pink tinged. From bogs and damp woods across Canada, south to New York and in the mountains to North Carolina and New Mexico.

G. *tesseláta*—A foot tall and densely downy with flowers loosely arranged. Native from Newfoundland to Manitoba to Minnesota and Maryland.

P. divaricáta

Description: The phloxes comprise a fairly large group, most of which is perennial. The leaves are usually lance-shaped or broadly so but may be either opposite or alternate, while the flowers are 5-petaled and rolled up in the bud. They are divided into two basic groups; the erect-stemmed ones from some of which our tall garden sorts are descended, and the dwarf or creeping kind, although the distinction is sometimes arbitrary and open to question.
Where They Grow: See below.
Blooming Season: See below.
Tall or Somewhat Erect Growing: *P. drúmmondi*—This is the annual phylox of our gardens. It grows to about 20 inches tall. The wild form is usually red-purple with a lighter eye and the only phlox with single leaves. It is native to fields and roadsides from the Carolinas to Florida and Texas. Easily grown from seed, especially if sown early in the North.

P. maculáta—Wild Sweet William. Perennial and somewhat smaller. Native from Quebec, Minnesota, southward to Georgia and Arkansas, it has lanceolate leaves up to 5 inches long and purple-spotted stems. The flowers are pinkish, purple or, rarely, white, and are borne in cylindric, many-flowered clusters.

P. paniculáta—There isn't any need to describe this one. It is the ancestor of many of our tall garden forms. Blooming season, July to September. A native of the open woods, it grows from New York to Iowa, south to Georgia and Arkansas. (A garden escape elsewhere.)

P. speciósa—(6 to 16 inches). It is somewhat woody at its base. The leaves are narrow but variable and up to 3 inches long. Flowers are pink or white and in loose clusters. It is at home in brushy and yellow pine country from California's Sierras and Coast Ranges to eastern Washington and Idaho.

Basically Low or Creeping Species: *P. subuláta*—Ground or Moss Phlox. Best-known creeper, it is native to dry rocky hills and banks from Maine to Michigan, south to North Carolina and Tennessee, forming broad mats. The leaves are sharp-tipped, linear, closely-set, and practically evergreen. The flowers are pink, purplish, or white in simple, few-flowered clusters, appearing generally in May and June.

P. alyssifólia—A plant with many hairy stems, often forming compact 4-inch tufts. The flowers are white, pink or lilac and held singly or in pairs on the stems. Blooming season May to July on open ground from Montana and the Dakotas into Colorado.

P. amoéna—Produces clusters of rosy blooms, but the leaves are flat, not needle-like as *P. subulata*. Perennial, 8 to 12 inches high, and native from North Carolina and Tennessee to Florida in dry, open woods.

P. bífida—Sand Phlox. A not-too-common native, it looks like moss phlox but is taller—a little more like wild blue phlox. The leaves are narrow, partly evergreen, and closely crowded. The pale purplish petals are split nearly to their base. Michigan to Iowa south to Tennessee and Oklahoma.

P. caespitósa—Has 2 to 6-inch somewhat woody stems and stiff, narrow, sharply-pointed leaves. The whitish, pink or lavender flowers are usually borne singly on the stems. Another from the yellow pine country of Washington and Oregon to Montana.

P. diffúsa—Grows 4 to 12 inches tall with prostrate or upcurving somewhat woody stems. The leaves are narrow and yellowish-green. The usually single flowers are pink, white or pale bluish. Native in woods and on rocky slopes in the Sierras and Cascades and eastward to Montana.

P. divaricáta—Wild Blue Phlox throws up 12-inch erect stems from creeping bases which root at the nodes. It spreads, but thinly compared with *P. amoena* and *subulata*. The petals are deeply notched at the edges, are pale blue or lavender, and appear April to June. From dry or damp, rocky, usually deciduous, woods, Quebec to Michigan and southward (pH 6 to 7).

P. hoódi—Forms cushions 1 to 2 inches tall with aul-shaped leaves that are cobwebby at the base. The white to lavender flowers are usually borne singly. Blooms some time April to June in heavy, clayey soil from California to Washington and North Dakota to Nebraska and Colorado.

P. nána—Canyon Phlox makes a loose tuft of leafy stems 4 to 12 inches tall clothed with narrow leaves. The two to six white, pink, lilac or purple flowers often have a pale eye. From the chaparral country of West Texas to Arizona.

P. ováta—Mountain Phlox varies in height from 10 to 20 inches depending upon location, often lying on the ground with only the tips turning up. An open grower with only a few pairs of leaves (long-stalked below, stalkless above). The flowers vary from pink to red-purple and appear between May and July in open woods and meadows, Pennsylvania to Indiana and south to Georgia and Alabama.

P. pilósa—From dry sandy woods and prairies, Connecticut to Manitoba, south to Florida and Texas. Like blue phlox, but the downy leaves are narrow, the plants are without basal runners and the flowers rosy, lavender or white.

P. stolonífera—Almost "round" leaves. Creeps madly, never staying put. Reddish-purple flowers, April to June. From damp woods, Pennsylvania to Ohio and Georgia.

P. woodhoúsei—Almost a dwarf shrub with thick, lanceolate leaves to 2 inches long. The pink or purplish flowers are often streaked in the center and have clefted narrow lobes giving a pinwheel effect. Found in open, rocky woods in Arizona and western New Mexico. Height 4 to 6 inches.

Culture: All are comparatively easy to grow, transplant well, are not fussy about soil, and most can be grown from seed sown in protected beds, if it can be obtained. However, they are usually divided after blooming and the creepers started from cuttings taken then. Preserve the phloxes. They are worth it!

Description: Low, slightly woody evergreen plants with long underground stems and shining, thickish leaves more or less in whorls or scattered along the short upright stems. The flowers, which are white or pink-tinted, 5-parted, and broadly cup-shaped, appear singly or in 1 to 8-blossomed clusters. The species reach a maximum of height of about 12 inches and bear capsule-like fruits which often last over winter in the dried form.

Where They Grow: Usually in dry, open acid woods, often under or near pines or other conifers. Europe, Asia and North America.

Blooming Season: June and July and into August in the case of the more northern plants.

C. maculáta—Striped Pipsissewa, sometimes also referred to as the spotted wintergreen but this leads only to confusion with the true wintergreen, a *Gaultheria*. A little more southern species, it is found from southern New Hampshire to Ontario, and Michigan south to Georgia and Alabama.

The chief difference between this species and *umbellata*, with which it often grows, is the handsomely marked evergreen leaves. These markings generally follow the location of the principal veins. The shape, too, is distinctive. Unlike the other, its leaves are widest in the stem-half and taper to a sharp point at the tip. A very neat and attractive plan at any season but never too plentiful and it rarely, if ever, makes a solid mat of any size.

C. ménziesi—Has ovate, toothed and sometimes mottled leaves up to 1½ inches long. The flowers are white and rather few. Inhabits the woods in California's Coastal Range and Sierras, to British Columbia and east into Montana. It is summer flowering and 2 to 6 inches tall.

C. umbelláta—Pipsissewa. Native from Canada's Atlantic provinces to British Columbia and Alaska, south to Georgia, Illinois, Utah and California, it is a hardy, dependable plant which comes up year after year. The leaves are narrowly wedge-shaped, 2 to 4 inches long, bluntly-pointed and tapering to the stem. The flowers are ½ to ⅔ inch across and readily show their relationship with the pyrolas or shinleafs with which they are often found along with lowbush blueberries, pink ladyslippers and true wintergreen or similar plants.

Culture: As we have mentioned above, the plants are denizens of the drier, open woods where the soil is well-drained and acid, averaging about pH 5. They need shade to survive, as well as a mulch of leaves, pine needles, or peatmoss over the roots. Transplanting is not easy at any season, and to be assured of success plants set out in the wild should be pot-grown.

The seeds are very fine and I know of no one who has had any appreciable success with them. However, the plants can be grown from cuttings by several methods. In one, the stems are cut off ¼ inch below the whorl of last year's leaves after the new stem growth has fully developed but not yet begun to harden, usually in early July. These lower leaves are cut off, leaving a greenwood cutting with a stub of old wood. The cuttings are then placed in sand or sand and peat in a coldframe. Keep the frame closed and the cuttings watered moderately. Some root by fall but most wait until spring. Then pot up and keep in pots until large enough to set out.

Opúntia humifúsa (O. vulgaris)

Cacti are a subject by themselves. One could devote a whole book to them, alone. Because of this and the fact that they are so many and varied, we are touching upon them most briefly and hope that we shall be forgiven by their devotees.

Surprisingly, there are even a few species which come all the way East such as that illustrated which the author has grown outdoors over 20 years and has used to describe culture.

Opúntia humifúsa—Prostrate and spreading, it makes almost solid carpets up to a yard or more across. The leaves are hardly visible little awls flat against the stem and soon drop off. However, to take over the duties of the leaves the jointed stems have become much enlarged into thick, flattened, pads.

In June and July appear golden blooms, 2 inches or more across, with 8 or 10 petals, crowned with many stamens. Each flower opens to the sun 2 or more days. In time they are followed by attractive red pear-shaped fleshy fruits which unfortunately for the plants are edible fresh or stewed. It grows in dry, sandy and rocky places from Massachusetts to Ontario and Minnesota, south to Georgia, Alabama, Missouri, and Oklahoma.

Comment: In spite of their thorns, these plants suffer at the hands of vandals, perhaps because the average person does not expect to meet a cactus in the East and the novelty is too strong for him. At any rate, the plants are not common and are rapidly becoming less so. This calls for action, for there are many places along the coast and inland where these plants could be re-introduced and restored for future generations.—And there is no reason why everyone cannot have some part in it.

Culture: Given a dry, sandy, rocky, or gravelly place where drainage is unobstructed, they will readily make themselves at home and produce sizable plants. The soil reaction should, preferably, be neutral or nearly so and the plants given full sun for best results. Temperature does not seem to enter into the picture, for these can well stand it over a hundred on hot summer days and are often exposed to 40° below zero on the cold, windswept plains in the northwestern part of their range.

Propagation is possible from the seeds within the fruits. However, a still easier method exists. All one needs to do is break off some of the joints and stick them into the ground. They root readily. For faster growth a little loam may be incorporated with the sand so long as drainage is good.

Other Species: Besides the giant *Caṛnégiea gigántea* or saguaro and *Lemaireocéreus marginátus* or organ pipe which are too large for our readers, there are numerous smaller cacti such as the teddybear, Christmas and jumping chollas, pronounced chóyas, (*Opúntia bigelóvi, leptocaúlis* and *fúlgida*) and the barrel cactus (*Ferocáctus wislizéni*) and their many relatives whose culture is relatively easy. These latter cacti are all western species.

Purple Coneflower—*Echinácea purpúrea* and Relatives

Description: A stout long-lived perennial with strong but little-branched 3 to 5-foot stems and rough, ovate, toothed leaves placed alternately on the stem. The flowers are daisy-like but larger (up to 5 inches) with brownish-purple "petals" that bend backward as they age and a large high dark crown. Not only do the plants bloom a long time, but the flowers are particularly long-lasting, sometimes remaining in good condition a month or more. Except for the purplish hue they might easily be confused with the similiar but shorter-petaled, lower-crowned black-eyed Susans.

Where They Grow: Generally in dry woods, fields, and prairies from Virginia to Michigan and Iowa, south to Georgia and Louisiana.

Blooming Season: July, August, and sometimes later.

Other Species: *E. angustifólia.* Narrow-leaved Coneflower. A much smaller plant, growing to 2 feet, clothed with long, narrow leaves. The flowers, too, are smaller, less showy, and light purple. Native to dry slopes and limestone barrens from Montana to Colorado to New Mexico and Texas, it is nowhere near so desirable. Flowers May to August according to location.

E. pállida—It grows to a height of about 3 feet. The leaves are narrow and not toothed. The rose-purple flowers rather large (up to 5 inches). Like both of the preceding species, white forms are occasionally found. Except for isolated spots farther east, its range is from Montana and Nebraska to Alabama and Texas, blooming usually June and July.

E. paradóxa—This one kicks over the traces by having orange-yellow rays. It is found primarily in Arkansas and Missouri in like habitats.

Culture: All these are easily grown. Except for *E. angustifolia* which prefers limestone areas, they are not fussy about soil acidity. Also, they will tolerate dry, sun-baked locations but do better in good rich prairie soils. Transplanting is easy at almost any season, although early spring and late fall are best. Dig a circle around the plant and lift with a large ball.

Propagation is likewise easy. The seeds do not germinate reliably but they will germinate. Rather than waste them on open ground, plant in flats or pots of finely-screened soil to which leafmold or peatmoss and sand has been added. Cover lightly. Transplant to flats and again to the open soil when the plants are large enough.

A satisfactory method is to dig plants up in late fall or early spring and separate down to single stems. After a year in a coldframe or planting bed, they are ready to re-establish themselves in suitable locations in the wild.

R. odorátus

Description: Perhaps it is unfair to select only two out of the more than 200 species and varieties native to or naturalized in this country. However, these two are distinct and, I believe, best suit our purpose as wild flowers. **Blooming Season:** June to September in the case of the first and June to August for the other, both ripening their fruits about a month later. **Species:** *R. odorátus*—Purple-flowering Raspberry is an attractive plant in its place, the borders of woodlands where it can peek out and get a little occasional sun. However, it seems to like the protection of overhanging growth to open, dampish, rocky places where the soil is at least moderately acid (pH 5.0 to 6.0). In such situations, it has much to recommend it for roadside and sanctuary restoration but if given a place where life is too easy, it becomes coarse, loses much of its beauty, and tends to be a pest.

It makes a large plant, 3 to 5 feet tall, with broad leaves easily confused with those of the striped mountain maple or moosewood. Unlike most raspberries, prickles are almost absent but the stems are covered with reddish-brown bristly hairs. The flowers are large, 5-petaled and very rose-like. At first they are a deep crimson pink and then turn more or less magenta—but surprisingly pleasant in their natural surroundings. The scattered fruits are typical raspberries but a little tasteless. Nova Scotia to Michigan south to Georgia.

Culture: Simple. Give them a similar location and they are happy. Set them out any time of the year, cutting the stem back about one-half to reduce evaporation unless done in early spring or late fall. Start new plants from seeds sown outdoors, by division of the clumps or from stem cuttings which root readily. Native from eastern Canada to Michigan, south to Georgia.

R. chamaemórus—Bake-apple or Cloudberry, a low, trailing creeper 3 to 9 inches high, with more roundish leaves and single, white strawberry-like flowers about an inch across. The berries are at first a pale wine-red, but when ripe turn an amber color and possess a delicate flavor.

A northern plant, it is found in acid peat at the tip of Long Island, the mountain tops of Upstate New York and New Hampshire and Maine. Farther north it ranges from Newfoundland to the Pacific Coast as well as Greenland, Alaska, and the Old World.

Where acid peat bogs exist it will grow along with blueberries, cranberries, pitcherplants, sundews, arethusas, Labrador tea and *Kalmia polifolia*. Set it fairly high but where its roots can still get steady moisture and propagate from seeds sown on moist sphagnum on top of peat and sand, or from runners rooted in the latter mixture.

Early Saxifrage and Blue-eyed Grass
Saxífraga virginiénsis and *Sisyrínchium angustifólium*

Saxífraga virginiénsis

Description: A small plant with a basal rosette of leaves vaguely similar to mustard greens and a 6- to 14-inch stem covered at the top with a mist of tiny white flowers almost as small as the cultivated baby's-breath. The leaves are 2 to 3 inches long, oval, toothed, and blunt-pointed. Not a well-known or showy plant but an interesting one.

Where They Grow: Wet or dry rocks and gravelly slopes, either open or shaded, from Quebec to Manitoba, south to Georgia and Oklahoma.

Blooming Season: With the first flowers of spring, usually April or May.

Culture: Rather easy to please so long as the site is rocky, with a cool, moist root-run and good drainage. It apparently is not fussy about soil acidity and thrives in either sun or shade. It is easily transplanted at almost any season. I well recall one plant uprooted during the hot summer weather and after two days without attention replanted with no obvious harm.

It self-sows freely if allowed to and is easy to raise from seed sown in pots or scattered with a little finely sifted soil. It can also be increased by division or cuttings soon after flowering. Blooms slightly ahead of both *Anemonella* and *Anemone quinquefolia* and worth saving from the path of construction for its misty mounds of tiny white blooms.

/————/

Description: Botanists now recognize many species of *Sisyrinchium* but for our purposes this one will serve as an example. It is a small plant, 4 to 14 inches high, looking like a tuft of stiff grass. The stem is simple or little-branched except at the top, where it bears a number of deep violet-blue, 6-petaled flowers about ½ inch wide which open only in sunshine. After the flowers come tiny ball-like seed-pods ¼ inch across.

Where They Grow: Meadows, grasslands, and open woods in damp, neutral to fairly acid soil from Newfoundland to Minnesota, south to Florida and Texas. Others are spread over the country.

Blooming Season: May to July.

Culture: One of our most attractive small plants and one of the easiest to grow. It can be found in both light and moderately heavy soils but prefers the former. It is easily dug up in clumps at any season and transplants readily even in full bloom. In fact, that is about the only time one can find wild plants, for at other times they pass for a grass. It seeds freely and soon makes small patches with or without human aid.

The Showy Orchis—*Órchis spectábilis*

Description: Truly a plant that lives up to its name. From a thick, short root-stock and fleshy roots it throws up a sturdy-looking plant with 2 more or less oval leaves somewhat like those of the pink ladyslipper but a dark glossy green. They usually measure from 4 to 8 inches long and 2 to 4 inches wide.

From between these leaves there rises a 5 to 12-inch thick, 5-angled terminal spike bearing 3 to 10 attractive lavender and white flowers about an inch long. After the blooming is over their place is taken by longish capsules full of tiny seeds, fine as powder.

Where They Grow: Generally they are found in rich moist woods often of mixed hardwoods and conifers, and occasionally with such plants as the purple trillium and maidenhair fern. Their range runs from Quebec to Minnesota, south to Georgia, Alabama, Tennessee, Arkansas and Kansas.

Blooming Season: This usually comes in May or June—or as late as July in the far northern parts of their range and about the same time as the purple trillium.

Other Species: Related, but nowhere near so showy, is *Orchis rotundifólia*, the Small Round-leaved Orchis, a more northern orchid from the moist woods and bogs, Greenland to Alaska and south to Minnesota, Wyoming and New York. It is a much more slender species, reaching a height of only 10 to 12 inches and producing one single oval or nearly round leaf, 3 to 4 inches long. Often confused with the round-leaved habenarias, but they all have 2 leaves close to the ground. The 3 to 10 flowers are smaller (⅔ inch long) and whitish with purple blotches.

Culture: For an orchid *O. spectabilis* is comparatively easy to grow. It transplants easily when dormant in late fall or even in bloom if a large ball of soil is taken and if given a somewhat moist, rich, fibrous soil with a pH of about 5.5 to 6.5 and partial shade in mixed hemlock, beech, and maple woods it should survive. Like its near relatives, its chief pests are slugs and snails—which may be kept under control with such poison baits as Snarol—and humans.

Propagation, however, is again a stumbling block. I know of no one who has ever grown them from seed, which leaves as the only recourse to take advantage of natural division of the tuberoid-like roots whenever possible. This is slow and should be attempted only when the plants are dormant, preferably in late fall. In early spring they are striking out new roots.

O. rotundifolia is not so easily handled. Being more a northern bog orchid, it does not take so kindly to culture unless its natural conditions are duplicated closely. Transplanting should be attempted only while dormant or at other times only during periods of emergency as when in danger from construction. Since it comes from calcareous (limey) bogs, make sure the growing medium is neutral to only slightly acid and the location cool. Watch out for the same pests as above.

S. *virgínica*

Description: A large group characterized by 5 sepals and 5 pink-like petals of pink, red, or white, often notched or cut, and narrow opposite leaves.

Species: S. *acaúlis*—Found in the North and the mountains of New Hampshire, Colorado, Montana, and Washington forming low mats covered with pink. It grows well from seeds but flowers poorly at low altitudes even in many rock gardens.

S. *califórnica*—An attractive 20-inch, red-flowered species with 3-inch leaves of open brush lands and woods in California and southern Oregon. Easy from seed.

S. *caroliniana*—Wild Pink is a low and densely tufted sort growing from a thick perennial root in dry, rocky or sandy acid slopes and fields, in sun. Its flowering stems grow to a height of only 4 to 10 inches. The flowers are about an inch across, like the individual flowers of sweet William and a soft but fairly deep pink. Below the flower clusters the plants are clothed with sticky hairs. The leaves are 3 inches long, narrow, and widest near the tip. Maine to Alabama and west to Ohio and Missouri, blooming April to June.

S. *cucúbalus*—Bladder Campion. Perennial, it grows to a height of 3 feet, has broader leaves, blooms June to August, and prefers slightly moist meadows and roadsides. The petals are white and beneath them is a green inflated sac which children like to pop in their hands. (European) Newfoundland to British Columbia, Oregon, Kansas, Virginia.

S. *hoókeri*—Prostrate with white, pink or violet petals often narrowly divided in dryish places and wooded hillsides of northern California north especially in the Coast Ranges. Bloom time, April to June. Easy from seed or rooted stems.

S. *stelláta*—Starry Campion. Also 2 to 3 feet. Its flowers white, starry, and fringed, come in small clusters, dianthus-like. The leaves, which are broader, are found in 4's. A perennial in woods and clearings, Massachusetts to North Dakota, south to Georgia and Texas. June to August.

S. *virgínica*—Fire Pink. Flowers like S. *caroliniana* but dazzling scarlet. The stems reach about a foot but are weak and reclining. Like the above, it is perennial. It, too, is sticky, hairy, and produces similarly-shaped but slightly longer leaves below its deeply-cleft blooms in small, few-flowered clusters. Often woods and rocky slopes: Ontario to Minnesota, Oklahoma, Arkansas, and Georgia.

Culture: While the roots, especially of S. *caroliniana*, are difficult to dig without breaking off, it does not seem to matter greatly. Moving is best done when dormant but can be tried at other times. Seeds sown when ripe in a pot in a cold-frame germinate the first spring and may bloom the second.

149

Some More Westerners
Clárkia, Eschschólzia, Mentzélia

Description: Again three groups of plants are considered together, not because of any relationship but because they are handled the same. While there are other species of each, those below were selected both as representatives of the culture of each group and because they are the ancestors of present day garden flowers. All are annuals or are generally treated as such and may be used as mass plantings for bold color effects.

Species: *C. pulchélla*—An erect plant growing to 20 or 24 inches with linear to lance-shaped leaves 1 to 4 inches long. The flowers are bright pink to lavender, 3-lobed, the lateral lobes usually narrower than the middle one. Native east of the Cascades from British Columbia through Oregon and east to South Dakota blooming May to July in pine forests and brushy plains, in moderately dry locations from the valleys and foothills to about 6000 feet.

C. unguiculáta (C. élegans)—Slightly taller, it grows to 3 feet and bears pink to salmon or purplish (occasionally white) flowers with long slender basal claws and leaves sometimes ovate. It is common on dry slopes in California's Coast Ranges and Sierra foothills where it blooms May and June.

/———/

E. caespitósa (E. tenuifólia)—Grows 4 to 16 inches tall and has bright yellow petals reaching 1 inch in length. The leaves may be all near the base or some scattered on the stems. At home in the grasslands of the Sierra foothills, in central to southern California.

E. califórnica—California Poppy. The best-known of the species, it covers the open hillsides from southern California into Washington and Vancouver Island. The deep orange to light yellow petals range from 1 to 2½ inches in length on stems 12 to 24 inches tall. Though usually considered an annual it can be perennial under favorable conditions. The State Flower of California.

/———/

M. líndleyi—Evening Star. Also known as *Bartónia aúrea*, it grows 1 to 3 and 4 feet tall and can become a rather straggling annual. The flowers which may appear March to June in the wild, are fragrant and quite attractive. Up to 3 or more inches across, they have a tuft of golden stamens in the center and an interesting point on each golden petal. They bloom in March to June on sunny, rocky canyon slopes from 500 to 2000 feet in California's Sierras and southern Coast Ranges, opening in the evening and remaining open in the morning.

Culture: Scatter the seeds in any reasonably good soil in full sun or light shade in spring; the last two groups, in particular, where they are to bloom since they do not lend themselves readily to transplanting, rake in lightly, tamp the surface gently and keep from drying out by covering or misting until germination takes place. Thin for spacing, if they come up too thickly. Particularly in the milder parts of the country they may also be sown in the fall for earlier blooming. If conditions are favorable, they may also self sow.

The Dependable Spiraeas—*Spiraéa*

Description: Here we have a trio common, attractive and very easily-grown perennials. No one who has picked blueberries or trampled the summer fields and woods can fail to have seen these fine, foolproof plants. Tall, woody and producing white or pink spire-like blooms, they cannot be mistaken in the summer landscape.

Where They Grow: From the Maritime Provinces to Saskatchewan and Manitoba, south to North Carolina in not-too-dry or overly-rich soil along roadsides and in abandoned fields and pastures.

Blooming Season: July and August, sometimes into September.

Species: *S. latifólia*—Meadowsweet grows to a height of 3 to 4 feet, producing straight, smooth reddish stems, little-branched until they reach the top. The leaves are light green, elliptical, nearly smooth, alternate, tooth-edged, and 2 to 3 inches long. At the top of the stem is a loose, branching pyramid of small, closely-crowded pink or whitish blooms. The individual flowers remind one in a rough way of miniature apple blossoms with prominent reddish stamens.

This is one plant that can hold its own even in pastures, for grazing animals don't care for its bitter, astringent taste. Too bad other wild flowers don't all share this property! Along with the highbush blueberries in the hilltop pastures, it also associates with the bayberries, favorites of the Christmas candlemakers, and the shy, acid-loving wood lily.

Closely allied to it and sometimes confused with it is the willow-leaved, white-flowered *S. álba* (*S. salicifólia*) which covers more or less the same range but is less abundant, probably because it confines itself primarily to lower, damper places.

S. tomentósa—Hardhack or Steeplebush. This is perhaps the next best known. Like the others, it is a woody perennial, attractive and "tough as nails." The stems rise directly from the rootstocks and generally remain unbranched right up to the flower spike. This latter is much narrower and more spire-like than *S. latifólia* and is made up of smaller flowers which are usually pink or purplish (rarely white).

The leaves are roughly of the same shape, seem to point upward and are definitely white and woolly beneath. The bark is red and clothed with a rusty wool which readily rubs off. Although many of the books place this plant in low wet ground, I have found it equally effective and happy on sterile hillside pastures. Companion plants are about the same.

Culture: Both major species above like the same conditions, some moisture but with good drainage and an acid not-too-fertile soil. They also like full or a generous amount of sun. To be honest, these plants are no friends of the farmer because they are tough to cut and are not affected by pasturing cattle. But kept where they belong, along the roadsides or open, grassy, non-tillable rocky places, they are a welcome part of the landscape.

They grow easily from seeds sown as soon as ripe in beds outdoors and moved to their permanent locations the second spring. If desired, they can also be propagated by division of the clumps and from summer cuttings, preferred methods for particularly well-colored sorts.

The Spring Beauty—*Claytónia virgínica* and Others

Description: A charming, delicate-appearing but hardy perennial that reaches a height of only 5 to 12 inches. Stem leaves are narrow, almost grass-like, 5 to 7 inches long and on opposite sides of the stem, about a half-way up. The plant grows from a tiny tuber or corm buried several inches deep and produces several graceful 5-petalled white or pinkish blooms, with darker veins ½ to one inch across. Following them come tiny seed capsules, and once these have ripened the plants disappear until the following spring.

Where They Grow: Denizens of moist, open, usually non-evergreen woods from Newfoundland to Minnesota south to Georgia and Texas.

Blooming Season: April or earlier in the South, May in the North.

Other Species: *C. caroliniána*—Very closely related and similar except that the stem leaves are considerably broader and more trowel-like. Likewise the flowers are fewer and earlier and the bulb often thicker. Its range is from Newfoundland to Saskatchewan, south to Minnesota, North Carolina and Tennessee. Less plentiful along the coast than the Middle West, where it is quite common.

C. lanceoláta—Showiest of the western species, it reaches a height of 6 inches, has both basal and stem leaves and pink (or yellowish) flowers. At home in moist woods, along streams and on alpine slopes, norther California into Canada, Wyoming and New Mexico.

Culture: Easily-grown little plants in almost any good soil where there is a reasonably good supply of humus and moisture. They are not fussy about soil acidity but seem to do best in one nearly neutral or only slightly acid (pH 6 to 7). They make ideal plants to establish in quantity in the high shade of open, park-like deciduous woods where, once started, rapidly spread.

Transplanting is easy at almost any time, provided large deep sods are taken, which means that they are easily rescued from the path of construction jobs. When the plants have died down, the pea-sized corms can be recovered by screening the soil. When replanting, set them about 3 inches deep and a few inches apart.

If seed can be obtained, plant it just under the surface in pots of ordinary garden soil, if necessary, in fall or spring, and cover with glass to retain moisture. The following fall, screen out the tiny corms and replant farther apart in flats. Left to themselves, they self-sow freely, and seedlings come up almost everywhere. Rapid spreaders, they may be picked reasonably freely. However, the flowers do not last.

Swamp Pink—*Helónias bulláta*

Description: If you are one who already knows this handsome plant, you are unusual, for attractive though it be, surprisingly few people know it. A hardy perennial, it grows from a stout, tuberous rootstock which, early in the season while everything else is bleak, throws up a 1 to 2-foot hollow stalk crowned with several inches of blooms. The flowers themselves are small, star-like heliotrope-scented, and a rosy-lilac with 6 blue anthers for contrast. In all, there are 30 or more blooms, making a dense cylinder of color.

The leaves are basal, strap-like, 5 to 12 inches long and form dense evergreen rosettes that often last until the next spring.

Where They Grow: Native to acid bogs and swamps from New Jersey and southern New York south in the mountains to Georgia, it is rare and strictly local in nature.

Blooming Season: Early April in the southern part of its range to early May at the northern limits.

Culture: An easily-grown, easily-satisfied plant for boggy or swampy areas and one which will grow well north of its natural range. Since it is an early spring bloomer, transplanting is best done in early fall, so that it may become sufficiently re-established by spring.

It will grow in both glaring sun and fairly dense shade. If found in the sun, it will almost always be perched on the hummocks in a wet, acid sphagnum bog. If in the shade, it may even be found on rich, rather dry ground.

Another favorable characteristic is its ability to multiply rapidly from offsets. A single plant may give rise to as many as 10 or 12 others by fall. Under cultivation it is less prolific with its seeds but, since it increases itself so rapidly otherwise, it is hardly worth bothering with seeds anyway.

Seeds, if used, should be sown on a ½-inch layer of moist chopped sphagnum over a good, well-drained but moisture-retaining mixture of soil, sand and peat acidified with a little sulfur if necessary.

It is a plant worth restoring to its former haunts and, because of its scarcity, it might be well to introduce it into favorable locations even as far north as Boston. (It has been grown in the Pacific Northwest.)

Further, it forces readily in pots indoors and is ideal for use in connection with conservation exhibitions and displays. After it has served its purpose, the swamp pink can be replanted out of doors with little setback as soon as the weather moderates.

Trailing Arbutus or Mayflower—*Epigaéa répens*

Description: Once quite plentiful, the Mayflower of our eastern woodlands is now seldom seen in many of its old haunts—if they, themselves, still remain what with overpicking and the relentless march of our so-called civilization. However, scuffling through the old leaves of the previous year in early spring will still occasionally reveal the stiff, oval leaves, 1 to 3 inches long and about half as wide; the hairy, creeping, half-woody stems and the small, fragrant pink or white tubular flowers clustered at the ends of the branches. The plant is evergreen and, given a fighting chance, has been known to make patches several feet across but such are almost never seen these days.

Following the flower comes the fruit, somewhat 5-lobed, fleshy, hairy, and about ¼ inch in diameter, which splits open when ripe, exposing the fleshy interior.

Where They Grow: In spite of its being so closely allied with New England in the minds of a large part of the public, the trailing arbutus is native from Newfoundland to Saskatchewan and south to Iowa, Mississippi and Florida. It is not a tolerant plant and definitely prefers acid, sandy or rocky soils along the edges of woods and especially under or near pines.

Blooming Season: An early spring-blooming plant generally found in April or May over most of its natural range.

Culture: Unlike that of most of the wild flowers we have already discussed, the culture of trailing arbutus is not easy. First, because it produces such long trailing stems, it is difficult to pick without harm and more so to transplant. However, wherever construction threatens this plant it is a mistake not to try to move it. If large clumps can be loosened 2 to 3 inches beneath the surface with a spade or turf edger and then rolled up like sod, it is well worth-while attempting the transfer. If not, it is much better to move only the young plants standing alone and to take just cuttings from the large clumps. After moving, the soil around the plants should be well mulched with pine needles, decaying oak leaves, peat, or sawdust, and care taken that the plants do not dry out. The soil acidity should read pH 4 to 5.

To grow from cuttings, take the new growth in August or early September with a small heel of old wood attached. Place the ends in peatmoss, keep moist, and after about a month they should be sufficiently rooted to pot up in sandy, acid soil. Keep over winter with the pots plunged in a shaded coldframe. In June old plants can often be broken up and the poorly rooted stems treated somewhat as above or when time permits soil may be mounded over them to produce true layers. This, however, takes about a year before moving them is safe.

Seeds usually ripen the same time as wild strawberries. Bag the fruits to save them from ants and birds. Squeeze out the seeds and sow at once, covering only lightly with sphagnum dust or vermiculite and a pane of glass. Germination takes a month or more and growth is slow. Transplant as necessary. Blooming takes 3 years or more.

T. grandiflórum

Description: The trilliums comprise a large group and, as their name implies, their leaves and flower parts all come in 3's or multiples of 3. The fruit is a many-seeded berry, likewise divided into 3's. Much more important, however, is the fact that, as a group, they are easily grown and long-lived perennials. Their greatest weakness is the short flower stems. In order to pick the blooms it is necessary to take the leaves, too, and thus the plants are robbed of their means to manufacture food for the next year.

Where They Grow: In general, they prefer the rich, moist, humus-filled soil and shade of mixed deciduous and evergreen woods. A dozen or more are found east of the Mississippi, 5 in the far west, another 5 or 10 in Asia.

Blooming Season: Early spring, usually before leaves come on the trees.

Species: The following are, perhaps, the most important native species.

T. catesbaéi (T. stylósum)—Catesby's Trillium, a pinkish, drooping species from the southern mountains of North Carolina and Georgia. Plant on hillsides and look up at it for best effects. It seems to like a moist, acid soil and will grow in the north. Late.

T. cérnuum—Nodding Trillium. White, flowers often hidden beneath the leaves. New England to Minnesota, southward. Almost rhizomeless but easy. Slightly later than *T. erectum*.

T. eréctum—Purple Trillium. Common and ill-scented carrion-flower but attractive and a lusty grower not fussy about soil. Often under hemlocks, maples, and beeches. Very effective with *T. grandiflorum*.

T. fléxipes—(T. declinátum)—White to maroon. "Sweetly"-scented, with short stout rhizomes. Open deciduous woodlands, New York to Minnesota and Missouri.

T. grandiflórum—White or Great Trillium. One of the best and easiest to grow. Flowers large, white turning to pink with age. Plant 6 inches deep in near-neutral soil. Appreciates attention, responding in size and number. Quebec to Minnesota, south to Georgia and Arkansas in mixed woods. (Also a double form.) Same conditions as Christmas ferns, Solomon's seal.

T. lutéum—Yellow Trillium. Greenish-yellow with attractively-mottled leaves. Happy in loam and leafmold. Native from Alabama to Arkansas north to Kentucky and Missouri but does well in North. Lemon-scented.

T. nivále—Snow Trillium. Tiny, the earliest and smallest of eastern trilliums (to 6 inches). Seems to prefer somewhat drier neutral limestone soils. Pennsylvania to Kentucky and Nebraska.

T. ovátum—Large, white fading to rose. Easy in cool, peaty soil. A West Coast counterpart of *T. grandiflorum* but a little earlier.

T. undulátum

T. recurvátum—Prairie Trillium. Attractive but beauty more in mottled leaves than browish-red flowers. Easy-grower, reliable bloomer from rich woods, Ohio to Alabama, Mississippi and Arkansas.

T. rivále—Western Snow Trillium. Small. Earliest of western species. Like *T. nivale* but has pinkish to white flowers marked with purple. California and Oregon. Good for shady corners or pockets.

T. séssile—Stemless Trillium. Fairly large. Purplish to greenish flowers. Slightly fragrant. Moist woods. New York to Georgia and Mississippi and Illinois. Will grow in North. Variety *califórnicum* with mottled leaves now *T. chloropétalum.*

T. undulátum—Painted Trillium. Needs acid soil and cool, damp woods. Attractive but not as strong a colonizer as *T. grandiflorum.* Prefers company of clintonia, oxalis, goldthread, and miniature mountain cranberry. Nova Scotia to Manitoba, south to Georgia.

T. vaseyi—Rare but one of the best. Large and latest-blooming of all with red-purple reflexed flowers. From southern mountains. Sweetly scented.

Others include small, white *T. pusíllum*, *T. stamíneum* (both like lime), trailing *T. decúmbens*, green *T. víride* and Northwest's *T. petiolátum.*

Culture: As a group, trilliums are easy to handle, most of them growing from thick, fleshy roots or tubers which are both hardy and permanent where conditions are to their liking. They can be transplanted any time of year, if done carefully and a sufficiently large ball of soil is taken, but late summer and early fall are best, for then they are dormant. Set the tuberous roots 2 to 6 or 7 inches deep, according to size. While the soil appears to vary from neutral to real acid, pH 6 seems to keep many happy.

Trilliums can be grown from seed sown as soon as ripe in a sandy leafmold, kept moist, shaded and in a protected place under glass or outside. The seedlings generally appear the following spring and flowering begins the third year. Seeds not planted at once, may take a year longer to germinate. Clumps may also be divided when not in bloom.

Still another method is often possible with the more bulbous-rooted species. Numerous small "bulblets" may be produced in many cases by decapitating the parent "bulb" or cutting out a v-shaped ring around it between the old and the new growth, preferably after flowering in late spring. The following year the "bulblets" may be removed after blooming time and planted by themselves. They should commence blooming in another year or two, depending upon their size.

Most of the trillums can even be brought into bloom in pots indoors if given several months in a cold place for the roots to become established, and then kept cool, preferably not much over 50 degrees.

Chief pests are slugs and snails, both of which can readily be controlled by scattering a little Snarol or other metaldehyde bait between the plants.

Description: A large group of low perennial plants arising from usually deeply buried, long slender bulbs from which are generally produced two more or less oblong basal leaves with slender stems rising between, bearing the small lily-like flowers.

Where They Grow: Europe, Asia, Eastern North America, and particularly the area between the Rocky Mountains and the Pacific. Generally they are found in rich, deep, leafmoldy soil, slightly on the damp side in partial shade or full sun.

Blooming Season: Early spring.

Species: Of the species and varieties found listed the following appears to be the classification now agreed upon by most botanists.

E. americánum—Yellow or Eastern Troutlily. Not the showiest, but perhaps the best-known. It grows 5 to 12 inches high bearing the single lily-shaped yellow flower, tinged with brownish on the outside, above the attractive mottled leaves. Fairly common in moist, deciduous, or mixed woods and along banks in deep, rich soil (pH 5 to 7) from Newfoundland to western Ontario, south to Arkansas and Florida.

Flowering usually comes during trout season (late April) in the Northeast, hence its name. Among its companions are purple trilliums, false lily-of-the-valley, hepaticas, spring beauties, violets, and squirrel corn. Unlike most of the western species, it produces many offsets, producing large colonies but often with few flowers since the offset plants are too young to flower or the clumps too crowded.

E. álbidum—White Troutlily. Considerably scarcer in the eastern part of its range, but much more free-blooming and with leaves unmottled or less distinctly marked. A native of rich ground from New Jersey to Minnesota and south to Georgia and Texas. Seldom seen or offered by dealers but rather easy to grow even in the Northeast, where it spreads rapidly by seeds and offsets.

E. álbidum mesachóreum—A non-mottled sort from the prairies of western Iowa and Missouri to Kansas and Nebraska. It is frequently earlier blooming than *E. albidum*, lavender, non-reflexing, and less likely to produce offsets. It is little-known, generally found in open woods under oaks or hickories, and seems satisfied with an ordinary rich loam.

E. califórnicum—A handsome species from the open woods and shrubby hillsides of the Coast Ranges. The flowers are white, pink or a rich cream deepening to yellow at the base, large, prolific, and often several to a stalk above the mottled leaves. Several varieties are listed, such as Pink Beauty and White Beauty. It often does well in the East in rich moist soil with some shade.

E. citrínum—From the woods and brushy slopes of the Siskiyou Mountains of Oregon and Tuolumne County, California. Similar to *E. californicum* but somewhat dwarfer and whiter with more orange in the flower's center. It flowers in April and is also easy to handle.

E. grandiflórum—One of the finest of all. A true mountain species from the Rockies, Olympics and Cascades and one of the earliest bloomers, usually March in the East. The broad, glossy leaves are unmottled and the large, bright yellow flowers are produced many to a stem. Fairly easy to establish and generally dependable. Carl Purdy always considered the variety *robustum* still easier. Still others coming under this species, commonly known as the glacier lily, are *cóndidum (Idahoénse)* and *chrysándrum (parviflórum)*.

157

E. helénae (E. califórnicum bícolor)—From the general vicinity of Mount St. Helens, it prefers a moist soil. The fragrant flowers are usually white with a yellow base and the ovate to lanceolate leaves are strongly mottled. It is also offset-producing.

E. héndersoni—A handsome and reliable three-toned species from the wooded slopes and valleys of the Siskiyous along the California-Oregon border. Flowers a light purple banded with white and deep purple-maroon in the center.

E. hówelli—A slender, mottle-leaved sort with darker-centered yellow flowers that turn pinkish. Slightly later, it comes from roughly the same region as *E. citrinum*.

E. klamathénse—Native to northwestern California and neighboring Oregon, it produces one to three white and yellow flowers per stem later than most. The leaves tend to be narrow and little or unmarked.

E. montánum—The Avalanche Lily, beautiful but very difficult except in its restricted native habitat, the high mountain meadows or timberline "parks" of the Cascades and Olympics of Oregon, Washington and into British Columbia almost up through the snow. The flowers are pure white and orange at the base.

E. multiscapoídeum (E. hártwegi)—Coming from the hot, shrubby hillsides on the western side of the Sierra Nevadas, it seems to stand more sun and heat than most and suffers much less in transportation and storage. Also, unusual for a western species, it increases rapidly from offsets. The leaves are strongly mottled and the flowers similar to *E. californicum* but more yellow and one to several each on a separate stalk.

E. oregónum—The more or less creamy flowers are pale yellow inside with a yellow or red-brown base and the leaves are usually mottled. Denizens of the woods from northwestern California to British Columbia, they bloom in April or May.

E. propúllans—A little-known Midwestern species, from the rich soils of Minnesota and Ontario. Narrow and mottle-leaved, it produces small, solitary rosy blooms with yellow centers and multiplies by offsets as well as seeds.

E. púrdyi—Now properly listed as *E. multiscapoideum* according to the botanists.

E. purpuráscens—Usually smaller, with small, orange-centered, spreading yellow flowes crowded together in a group. The somewhat narrow leaves are wavy. Easily grown and attractive, it is found in moist, well-drained granite soils that turn dry in summer and fall in the coniferous forests of California's Sierra Nevadas.

E. revolútum—Handsome and truly the aristocrat of the group with its tall, strong stems and gracefully reflexed large flowers of white, pale lavender, or deep pink. From the heavy rainfall rgion of the low altitudes in the Coast Ranges from California into British Columbia, it stands a rich, moist loam. Purdy often found the plant completely submerged in winter and in soil still wet when ripe for digging. A very variable species according to locality, it has given rise to many beautiful varieties such as Pink Beauty, Rose Beauty, Johnsoni, Smithi, and Purdy's White.

E. tuolumnénsis—A large-leaved sort with flowers of golden yellow. The corms are large, cone-shaped and offset like tulips. The flowers are more bell-shaped, rather like a fritillaria. Native to a small area in the Sierra Nevadas of Tuolumne County in California and at an elevation of 3,000 feet but apparently acceptable over a wider area.

Culture: As a group, erythroniums are easy to handle and well worth restoring to their former haunts. They grow from corms like pencil stubs in size and shape, many double-ended. With a few exceptions the eastern species spread by underground offsets which may be readily separated and the western ones do not. Although the latter group are often very restricted in their natural range, they are amenable to more widespread growth, even to the East Coast if situations are to their liking. With all, the important point is to give them the same conditions under which they grow naturally. Plant them not less than 3 inches deep and the larger corms correspondingly deeper in loose, gritty, leafmouldy soil in not too much shade for the alpine species.

In addition to propagating some by use of offsets, all may be increased by means of seeds which ripen in June or thereafter. Sow in flats of ½ humus, ½ gritty soil. Germination often starts in the fall and the seedlings show by spring. Keep partially shaded and do not let suffer from drought. Of course, expect the seedlings, like the older plants, to die down for the summer. Some bloom the third year.

For conservation exhibitions, they are easily forced into bloom in pots indoors and may be set outdoors again when the weather moderates.

Twinflower or Deer Vine—*Linnaéa boreális americána*

Description: The twinflower is a delicate and beautiful little vine from the wooded areas of Canada and the northern states. It is a half-woody plant with slender trailing stems reaching a length of about 20 inches, threading its way and often making a dainty but continuous mat over the forest floor.

The flowers are tiny, nodding, pinkish bells always in pairs and found at the top of wiry stems 3 to 6 inches high. They are 5-lobed, ½ inch long, and fragrant. Following the flowers come small, nearly round, dry fruits containing 3 cells but with only one good oblong seed.

The leaves are evergreen, more or less opposite, rounded and well below the level of the flowers. The American sort is but a variety of the basic species found throughout northern Europe and Asia.

Where They Grow: From Greenland to Alaska, south to West Virginia, Indiana, the Dakotas, Colorado, and northern California in the New World.

Blooming Season: June to August, rarely a few in late autumn.

Culture: A native of the cool, moist woods, it can be re-established in preserves, parks, and similar places if care is taken to give it suitable surroundings. But without such conditions it is a waste of plants to attempt a planting.

It seems to grow best on moist slopes where drainage is good and water does not collect. Also, it should have shade and an acid mold (pH 4 to 5) into which its roots can run and its woody stems clamber over mossy logs. Generally, I have found it under such trees as balsam firs, arbor-vitae, white and black spruces, mountain and red maples, yellow birches, mountain ash, and a few scattered aspens. Among its smaller companions are bunchberries, false lily-of-the-valley, clintonias, starflowers, painted trilliums, and goldthread. Plants collected from the path of construction may be taken at any time provided that large sods can be moved undisturbed. Otherwise, it is best to rely upon pot-grown plants so they can be moved without disturbance of the roots.

Propagation: This is not so difficult as one might think. While it is possible to raise them from seed, I know of no one who has made a practice of it. Growing them from cuttings, 3 to 5 inches of stem, is much quicker and easier with such small plants. These may be taken in spring or early summer and placed upright into moist sand and peatmoss (half and half), leaving the top third sticking out, in a coldframe. They may be in flats or directly in the bed of the frame. Do not let them dry out. They should be sufficiently rooted to pot up into the growing soil in 3 to 6 weeks. Cuttings taken in January have also been successful in a cool greenhouse.

Two Dainty Groundcovers—*Cóptis* and *Gaulthéria* (*Chiógenes*)

Description: Two small but attractive groundcovers. Though unrelated in appearance or botanically, they are listed here together because they are often found growing together and over essentially the same range.

Where They Grow: Both are inhabitants of the acid bogs and cool, moist woods from Labrador to British Columbia, south to Minnesota and in the mountains to North Carolina and Tennessee.

Blooming Season: May to June or July, according to location.

Coptis groenlándica (*C. trifólia*)—Goldthread, a dainty creeping plant with lustrous, dark green evergreen leaves that are three-lobed, scallop-edged, and borne on longish stems. The flowers are about ½ inch across, 5 to 7-petaled, white, and resemble a small, solitary blackberry blossom. Perhaps still more characteristic, however, are the yellow threadlike roots which are found just under the surface, in the acid humus.

C. laciniáta—Western Goldthread. In moist woods and on wet cliffs in the Coastal Ranges of upper California to mid-Washington, it bears small, whitish flowers on 6-inch leafless stems. Its twice-divided basal leaves are long-stalked. Some plants lack pistils, hence cannot fruit.

Culture: In addition to its companion on this same page, it also often is found in the company of the miniature mountain cranberry, bunchberry, twinflowers, and the oxalis, which furnish a key to its desired growing conditions. It is not difficult to transplant at almost any season but it must have a cool, always slightly moist, acid (pH 4 to 5), humus-filled soil and, when not in cool or mountain country, shade primarily of evergreens.

Propagation is readily effected by division in spring. It can also be started from root cuttings taken at the same time, planted in acid peat and kept well watered as well as shaded. Seed sown as soon as ripe germinates the first spring and often produces flowering plants by the following year. Keep in pots in slat-covered coldframes until large enough to set out.

/———/

Gaulthéria hispídula—Creeping Snowberry. One of the daintiest members of the Heath Family and one of the smallest of all the groundcovers, it is characterized by slender red-brown trailing stems which root at frequent intervals. The leaves are evergreen, shaped like those of the garden thyme and set at right angles to the stem. The typical heath's tiny flowers, which are white, bell-shaped, and nestled in the axils of the leaves, are followed by equally tiny white berries.

Culture: Like its companion, above, the creeping snowberry is not difficult to move at any season, but one must be certain that its new home will be to its liking first. To do otherwise is to court failure. A rotten stump in a somewhat moist balsam, spruce, or hemlock woods is often a good starting place when re-establishing this plant. While it spreads well if it is happy, it never smothers other plants.

It can be readily propagated by cutting stems into sections, planting them in acid peat in the fall and wintering in a coldframe or greenhouse just above freezing. But they must have ventilation, constant moisture, and partial shade. They are not fast-rooting. Also, they can be grown from the berries. Squash them and plant in peaty soil. It takes at least 2 years to produce plants large enough for setting out.

The Violets—*Vióla*

V. canadénsis

Description: A very large group of usually small plants, in many cases, early-blooming and inhabitants of moist places. However, they vary greatly. About the only universal characteristic is the 5-petaled flower, the lower petal of which projects backward as a spur. The seeds are borne in capsules which split into 3 parts and squeeze out the seeds when ripe. In addition, many also produce cleistogamous flowers (which never open) near the base of the plant. These blooms fertilize themselves and often yield more seeds than the regular ones.

Species: There are so many it would be impossible to even think about including them in a book of this scope. However, those selected comprise a representative group. First, the blues and purples.

V. conspérsa—Dog Violet. Purple as those below but a low plant, only 2 to 6 inches tall, it has somewhat paler flowers and leaves that are round to heart-shaped. However, though showy and borne above the leaves, the flowers are not particularly good for picking, since they are produced upon short axillary stems. Native to meadows, damp woods, and bottomlands, it grows from the Gaspe Peninsula to Minnesota, south to Georgia, Alabama and Missouri, blooming May to early July.

V. cullláta—Blue Marsh Violet. This and *V. papilionacea* are perhaps the commonest and best known of the clan. A tufted plant arising from a stout rhizome, its leaves and stems are smooth. The former are broadly ovate and with margins strongly rolled in when young. The flowers are violet blue with a darker throat and are held well above the leaves. A denizen of moist meadows, woodlands, and streamsides, it ranges from Newfoundland to Ontario and Minnesota, south to Nebraska, Arkansas, and Georgia, blooming April to July according to location.

V. flétti—Here is one that dares to be different. It has purple-tinted succulent leaves and purplish petals that are yellow at their bases. Blooming is between June and August. Home is rocky crevices in Washington's Olympic Mountains.

V. papilionácea—Common in low wet ground from Massachusetts to North Dakota, Wyoming and Colorado, south to Georgia and Oklahoma. The flower color is not so blue as *V. cucullata* and it more often produces purple-veined white forms. It differs from that species chiefly in its larger leaves, which are often higher than the flowers.

V. sagittáta—Arrow-leaved Violet. A small plant with deep green arrow-shaped leaves sometimes partly scalloped and growing from a stout rootstock. Both the leaves and the rich violet-purple flowers with white centers rise directly from the ground, the latter being equal to or taller than the leaves. Generally in wet meadows or dried sandy borders from Maine west to Minnesota, south to Georgia and Texas.

The white violets comprise an interesting group, a few representative ones being:

V. blánda—This is the Sweet White Violet, a small dainty plant growing 3 to 5 inches tall and bearing tiny fragrant purple-veined flowers in April and May. Its leaves are olive green, somewhat rounded and on shorter stems than the flowers. A plant of rich, chiefly deciduous, woods from Quebec to Minnesota south to Maryland and Tennessee and in the mountains of Georgia, it is one of the favorites of very small children.

V. canadénsis—Canada or Tall White Violet. One of the tallest and showiest of our violets, it sometimes reaches a height of 18 inches and bears its purplish-backed yellow-centered white flowers well above the leaves but upon comparatively short stems arising from the leaf axils. The leaves are more or less heart-shaped, tapering to a decided point. It is one of the longest-blooming violets, producing flowers from April to July and to a lesser extent to October. An excellent subject for the home wild garden as well as woods restoration. Newfoundland to Alaska, south to Oregon, Alabama, Iowa and Arizona.

V. lanceoláta—The Lance-Leaved Violet. One of our most distinctive species with its long, narrow, slightly scallop-edged leaves. The flowers are white, veined with purple on the 3 lower petals and long-stemmed, arising directly from or near ground level. It is also a rather spreading plant increasing rapidly from stolons as well as from numerous cleistogamous flowers. Blooms April to June and is common in moist ground from Maine to Florida and west to Minnesota and Texas. Variety *vittata*, with still narrower leaves, inhabits the wet pinelands from New Jersey to the Gulf.

V. pállens—Northern White Violet. A native of the mossy bogs, wet meadows and springy woods from Newfoundland and Labrador to Alaska south to North Carolina and Alabama (in the mountains), Iowa and Montana. Its leaves are small, broadly ovate to nearly round, pale green and noticeably shorter than the somewhat fragrant white flowers.

V. palústris—This violet has no erect, leafy stem. Its roundish leaves are long-stalked and come from the base as do the white to lilac flowers which appear between May and July. Found in meadows and moist, brushy places from northwestern California into Canada, it propagates readily by division, since it spreads by runners.

Among the better-known yellows we have several that are well worth preserving.

V. núttalli—This one differs from most because of its 3-inch ovate to lanceolate leaves. The flowers are yellow, the upper petal sometimes brownish to the back and the lower three with brown-purple lines. Blooms come April to July in dry, open woods and meadows from northern California to British Columbia, east to the Dakotas, south to Oklahoma and Arizona.

V. pedunculáta—More mat-forming than usual in violets. The leaves are ovate to triangular. Sometimes called the Yellow Pansy Violet because the flowers are like small, orange-yellow pansies. Flowers February to April on grassy slopes from Baja California north into the Coast Ranges and Sierra foothills.

V. pubéscens—Downy Yellow Violet. A tall showy plant very much like V. canadensis but with yellow flowers. The leaves, too, are somewhat similar and the flowers axil-borne. Its blooming season is April and May. A native of the rich, deciduous woods, it grows from Maine to North Dakota, south to Oklahoma and Georgia.

V. rotundifólia—Round-leaved Violet. A very early but relatively inconspicuous sort found on woodland floors and rocky hillsides in cool, damp or fairly dry situations. The leaves are small at first but by mid-summer are 2 to 4 inches across and lie flat on the ground. Its range is Quebec to Ontario, south to Georgia and Tennessee. Blooms April and May.

Of a much more unusual nature are the cut-leaved sorts:

V. lobáta—A yellow-flowered birdsfoot best describes this violet, although the leaves are not as finely cut as *V. pedata*, usually five to seven-lobed. It blooms April to July, according to location, in open woods in the Coast Ranges from southern California into southern Oregon.

V. palmáta—Palmate-leaved Violet. Somewhat similar but not so deeply cut and with smaller flowers of bright light violet or, at times, white. It grows in dry ground, in wooded places from Maine to Minnesota south to Florida and Mississippi.

V. pedáta—Birdfoot Violet. One of the most beautiful violets. The plant is small, tufted and the leaves so deeply cut they resemble a bird's foot. The flowers are blue-violet to lilac and are the largest of all, often measuring an inch across. Occasionally, 2-toned ones are found. A plant of dry sandy, acid soil often near pines, it blooms with the pink ladyslippers and lupines. Maine to Minnesota, south to Florida and Texas.

V. shéltoni—Another yellow-flowered cut-leaved species but with finely-cut bluish-green leaves (purplish beneath) that remind one of a dwarf bleeding heart. The flowers rise slightly above the leaves. It is at home in loamy soils in woods or brush from Baja California to Washington, blooming April to July.

Culture: Practically all violets are easy to grow if given conditions similar to those from which they come. With a few exceptions, as indicated above, this usually means a rich, humus-filled moist soil, only slightly acid and in partial shade either from trees or taller plants.

Those that make several-stemmed clumps may be divided at almost any season—after blooming preferred—and all can be grown from seed without difficulty. The only hard part is to get the seed before it scatters but a patient search at the base of the plants will usually disclose some. If necessary, transplanting can be done at any season, provided a good ball of soil is taken.

The Waterlilies—*Nymphaéa, Núphar,* and *Nelúmbo*

Description: See below.
Where They Grow: See below.
Blooming Season: Summer months.
Species: First we shall deal with the genus *Nymphaea (Castália)*, true water-lilies, with horizontal or erect rootstocks and roundish leaves floating on the surface.

N. élegans—This is the Blue Water Lily found in the swamps of southern Florida to Texas. Like the other tropicals, its flowers are held well above the water.

N. mexicána—Although native from North Carolina to Florida and Mexico, it is hardy into New England if grown in mud that does not freeze. In the North it is not a strong grower and its natural increase is slow. The odorless yellow flowers are held above the water and the leaves are flecked with dark spots.

N. odoráta—The true, sweet waterlily common in shallow ponds and slow-moving streams throughout most of the United States and neighboring Canada. The leaves vary from 4 to 12 inches in diameter and the 3 to 6-inch, many-petaled, fragrant flowers may be glistening white or pinkish. Blooming season is June through August and the fleshy, ball-like fruits which follow ripen beneath the surface.

N. tetrágona—They Pygmy Waterlily is found in colder water locally from Quebec to Washington, south to Idaho, Michigan and Maine. The flowers are white, to 2½ inches across and the leaves are somewhat horseshoe-shaped. Growth comes from a short, vertical tuber. Hence, there is no rapid horizontal spread but seeds germinate well. An iron-clad species suitable to small, shallow areas.

N. tuberósa—Tuberous Pondlily. Found from Quebec to Minnesota, south to Delaware, Nebraska, Illinois, and Arkansas. Differs from *N. odorata* in its larger leaves (more often up to 12 inches) which are green on both sides, larger flowers (to 9 inches across) with broader petals and little or no fragrance. It multiplies rapidly from artichoke-like tubers which detach themselves from the parent rootstock.

/———/

Next comes *Nuphar*, yellow pondlilies, less attractive than the *Nymphaeas*. They have stout, creeping rootstocks and ovoid fruits ripening above water.

N. advéna—With slight variations, a native from New England to the Rockies and south to Florida and Texas. The leaves are less round than on the *Nymphaeas*, up to 12 inches long and 9 wide, and the globe-shaped yellow flowers are often held above the water. They have fewer petals and never really "open." Bloom June to September.

N. macrophýlla—A Florida species with erect or floating, round or elliptical leaves up to 16 inches long and lemon yellow flowers.

N. microphýllum—A slender northern species with small leaves (to 4 inches) and inch-wide flowers.

*N. polysépala*This has leathery, oval leaves that either float or stand above the water. The petals are short, greenish-yellow, sometimes tinged with purple. At home from northern California to Alaska and east to Colorado and South Dakota.

N. rubrodíscum—Believed to be a hybrid between *N. microphyllum* and *N.*

165

variegatum, it is found over the same range as the former. It is intermediate in size, has flat leaf stalks and red stigmas.

N. *sagittifólium*—Narrow-leaved, with small flowers. From southern Indiana and Illinois southward.

N. *variegátum*—Noted for its flat leaf stalks, many of its leaves float on the surface. It is found across Canada and south to Delaware, Ohio, Iowa and Montana.

/———/

Nelúmbo lútea—American Lotus. Hardy, with large leaves, large pale yellow cup-like flowers and showerhead-like seed pods well above the water. A rapid spreader from horizontal rootstocks, it ranges from Massachusetts to Ontario and Minnesota to Florida and Texas, taking several years to fully establish itself. It flowers July to September.

N. *nucífera*—A pink-flowered species from southeast Asia and Australia that has become naturalized in the United States, particularly in New Jersey. It is larger than N. *lutea* with leaves ranging from 1 to 3 feet across.

Culture: All do well in deep, fertile mud in slow streams and ponds, needing both sun and warm water to bloom (except *Nymphaea tetragona*). They are readily propagated by dividing the thick tuberous rootstocks in late September. Seeds may also be used if pods are covered with cloth bags to catch them. Scatter the seeds by dropping in balls of clay or cloth bags into water 1 to 5 feet deep or sow 1 to 2 inches apart in pots in water. Transplant as needed and set outdoors the following spring. Lotus seeds do better if filed before planting. Protect the plants with wire screening if necessary, to prevent muskrats from eating the tubers.

Wild Callas and Skunk Cabbages

Description: A miniature calla lily best describes *Cálla palústris* of the northern swamps. Like the cultivated calla (really a *Zantedeschia*) the bloom is a broad, almost open, spathe and the true flowers are confined to the short, fat, yellow-green spadix. Unlike the cultivated sort, however, the spathe is whitish on the top only, the reverse generally greenish.

The leaves, which grow about a foot tall, are long-stemmed, thick, glossy green, pointed, and usually broadly heart-shaped at the base. Following the flowers come the nearly globular, densely-packed clusters of red berries much like those of the Jack-in-the-pulpit but smaller. They ripen any time from June to August according to their immediate location.

Where They Grow: The wild calla is a plant of the cold swamps and bogs ranging from Newfoundland to Alaska south to New Jersey, Indiana and Minnesota. It is more common in the northern parts of its range.

Blooming Season: Flowering, of course, varies with the location and normally extends from late May into early July.

Culture: A rather easy plant for shallow ponds or pools, preferably in full sun, although it will stand some shade, and moderately acid soil. It grows from a slender creeping rootstock more or less on top of the mud, generally in water only a few inches deep. During the summer it sends out its rootstock and after it has produced its fruit the old stock rots away, leaving the new with a few white roots along its under surface. The following spring a bud at the end of this gypsy-like stock develops into the new plant and in turn rots after its mission is completed. Thus it has a tendency to spread.

Propagation may be accomplished by removing the seeds from the red berries as soon as ripe and planting them in boxes or flats of fine, silty, or mucky soil submerged a couple of inches beneath the surface. Transplant the seedlings as soon as they are large enough to move and again to their permanent quarters the end of the first growing season, making sure to set the stocks horizontally and not too deep. In general, this method of propagation may also be used on such other water plants as arrowheads, *Sagittárias*, and the sweet flag, *Ácorus cálamus*.

/———/

The same applies to the two species below, except that they should be kept moist but not permanently submerged. In addition, however, they also be readily propagated by division, if one does not mind their "fragrance."

Symplocárpus foétidus—Eastern Skunk Cabbage. Unlike most plants, the whole flower is formed underground in the fall. In the spring it comes up through the soil around it. The actual flowers are found on the dome-shaped spandix which is surrounded by the pointed, red-mottled spathe just poked out of the soil and which, in turn, withers when the cabbage-like leaves appear. It blooms February to May in swamps and wet woods, Quebec to Manitoba, Georgia, Illinois and Iowa.

Lysichitum americánum—Western Skunk Cabbage is more attractive and is characterized by a yellow spathe standing up above the soil on a stem. Also, the leaves are ovate to lanceolate and 1 to 4 feet long. It blooms April to July in swampy places from Montana to northern California and Alaska.

Wild Geranium—*Geránium maculátum*

Geránium maculátum

Description: An easily-grown, reliable perennial growing from a stout root-stock to a height of about 1 to 2 feet. The flowers are 5-petaled, 1¼ inches across, a magenta-pink that is not unattractive in its natural surroundings, and come in clusters similar to those of the pelargoniums or so-called scented geraniums in cultivation. The stem leaves are short-stalked, opposite, 3 to 5 inches wide, nearly round and deeply 3 to 5-lobed into toothed and wedge-shaped sections.

Where They Grow: Moist woods, roadsides, and meadows, Maine to Manitoba, to Georgia and Arkansas in neutral or slightly acid soil.

Blooming Season: April to June.

Other Species: *G. bicknélli*—An annual or biennial with much more skeletonized leaves and unusual seed vessels which split open from the base and frequently bear the seeds at the tips of the sections. Open woods, Newfoundland to Alaska south to Pennsylvania, Utah and California.

G. califórnicum—Grows 1 to 2 feet tall with one or more thinly hairy stems. The pink or white petals are also hairy. Blooms June and July in damp woods and meadows, southern California through the Sierras.

G. caroliniánum—Carolina Geranium—Annual or biennial, many-branched, downy-stemmed and leaves somewhat less skeletonized, its flowers are pale, ½ inch across and in rather compact clusters. Dry rocky woods and waste places. Maine to British Columbia south to California and Florida. More plentiful in the South. Blooms May to August.

G. oregánum—16 to 32 inches tall, its leaves are 4 to 5 inches wide and the reddish-purple petals are fringed with hairs but not hairy on the surface. Found in woods, thickets and meadows, California into Washington west of the Cascades, blooming May to July.

G. robertiánum—Herb Robert. A handsome, ferny-leaved annual or biennial sort with long-stemmed leaves often 3 instead of 5-parted. The stems are 12 to 18 inches tall, and the flowers give way to long-beaked seed vessels. Stems and leaves are musky when bruised. Slightly moist rocky woods and ravines, usually on slopes in neutral or barely acid soil. Newfoundland to Manitoba, to W. Virginia, and Nebraska.

G. viscosíssimum—A western species from the prairies and open woods, South Dakota to British Columbia south to Nevada and California. Its identifying characteristics are the sticky hairiness of both flowers and leaves and the dense whitish coating this gives the leaves.

Culture: All are rather easy, although some, like *G. robertianum*, are more fussy about soil and therefore a little harder to grow than *G. maculatum*. All seed plentifully and germinate readily in pots in coldframes or prepared beds outside. The perennials also yield to division in spring or fall.

Wild Gingers—*Ásarum canadénse*, etc.

Description: Definitely not a showy or spectacular plant, the wild ginger is, nevertheless, one of our very best of ground covers for the deep shade. Broadly heart-shaped leaves, 3 to 6 inches across, growing in pairs, rise from a creeping, branching rootstock only slightly beneath the surface. From early spring, when they first appear, they make an attractive mat over the leaf-carpeted soil. The short-stemmed bell-like flowers, an inch or so broad and a curious brownish-purple color, are rarely seen, because they are borne so low they are often partially concealed by the leaves of the woods floor. The common name comes frm the aromatic rootstocks which are ginger-flavored and once used to settle stomach disorders.

Where They Grow: Wild ginger is a plant of the rich, slightly moist woods, growing in fairly deep shade from New Brunswick to Manitoba, south to North Carolina, Alabama, Arkansas and Kansas.

Blooming Season: This is generally in April or May according to the locality in which it is found but, unlike most plants, the flowers are very long-lived. They make up in lasting qualities what they lack in beauty, often persisting until the large, thick seeds have ripened.

Other Species: While the one here discussed is, perhaps, the most widely known, there are closely-related species.

A. *(Hexastýlis) arifólium*—Also evergreen, its leaves are more triangular and reach 5 inches long. The flowers are flask-shaped and about an inch long. Virginia, West Virginia and Kentucky.

A. *caudátum*—From shady woods in the Coast Ranges, Monterey Bay to British Columbia and Montana, its flowers are more visible and have long tails.

A. *hártwegi*—This has even longer tails than A. *caudatum* (3½ inches), more heartshaped, often mottled leaves. From the Sierras of mid-California into Oregon.

A. *lémmoni*—This one, from the wet places on the western slopes of the Sierras, has smaller leaves and no flower tails.

A. *(Hexastylis) shuttlewórthi*—Sometimes listed as A. *grandiflorum*, is also a more southern species from the mountains of Virginia, Tennessee, and North Carolina to Georgia and Alabama. It has curiously mottled evergreen leaves and is likewise a very desirable species. The flowers may reach 2 inches in length.

A. *(Hexastýlis) virgínicum*—A more southern species, it has smoother, ever-green leaves, more rounded and 2 inches across and flowers 1 inch long or less. Virginia to Kentucky, Georgia and Alabama.

Culture: Given a rich, slightly moist soil full of leafmold or other humus and shade, wild ginger will readily make itself at home. In a few years a small clump will cover a surprisingly large area. While it is not too fussy, it appears to prefer a soil with an acidity reaction of pH 6 to 7.

Transplanting may be done in early spring or fall. No special precautions are necessary, except in the case of fall-planted ones, a mulch of oak, beech, or other non-packing leaves is desirable to prevent heaving.

While it is possible to propagate plants by seeds, if they can be found, division of the roots in late fall is more practical. Cuttings taken in summer and rooted in sand are also successful producing plants quickly.

Culture of the lesser-known species is the same, except they appear to require a more acid soil, around pH 5.

Wild Lupine—*Lupínus perénnis* and Others

Description: One of the finest of our native wild flowers for growing in dry, sandy wastes. A hardy, erect perennial, it grows 1 to 2 feet high and is one of the few flowers providing blue in the landscape. The blooms are pealike, range from light through deep blue to purple, pinkish, and even white and are borne in handsome tapering spikes above gracefully cut leaves roughly similar to those of the horsechestnut. The fruits are pealike pods containing 5 or 6 hard seeds. **Where They Grow:** In poor, sandy, strongly acid soils from Maine to Minnesota, south to Florida and Louisiana, in company with pines, blueberries, bearberries, pink ladyslippers, on birdfoot violets over a large part of its range.

Blooming Season: Generally May or June.

Other Species: While the above, the common eastern species, may be one of the better-known ones to many readers, there is a much wider selection in the western parts of our country. In a general way, the same growing conditions and cultural methods apply to them also. However, there are some exceptions. For instance, some are annuals and may be propagated by seed only. Also, to say flatly that absolutely all insist upon an acid soil would not be the truth.

Now, to mention just a few representative species:

L. arbóreus—The Tree Lupine. Shrubby, showy and truly a giant, it grows up to 9 feet tall in the often shifting sands of coastal California. Its blooming season runs from March to September and, while the usual color is yellow, it is sometimes blue or lilac, or even two-toned. It has also been introduced and is being established farther north.

L. bréweri—Found in dry, stony places, often in coniferous forests, at mid- to high altitudes, it is prostrate and mat-forming. Its small leaves are silky or silvery and the flower heads are dense but, like the stems, short. The flowers are violet with a touch of white or yellowish, appear June, July or August, through the Sierras into Oregon.

L. chamissónis—Another (2 to 7 feet) from the sandy coastal beaches and dunes, this one is characterized by its shrubby nature and its silky or silvery-green leaves. However, the flowers are blue or lavender with a touch of yellow on the standards. At home in the southern two-thirds of California.

L. floribúndus—Growing 4 to 24 inches tall, silky with long-stalked leaves and long flower spikes, it is found over a considerably wider range than some of the others. It is found in dry places, often at high altitudes, from Montana to Oregon, south to Colorado, southern California, Arizona and New Mexico. Its color ranges from deep violet to whitish but is often a good blue.

L. formósus—An attractive white-flowered sort (sometimes also blue or violet), it is found throughout California and into the Southwest. Moderately tall, it grows to a height of 1 to 3 feet but often bends over and trails on the dry ground. The flowers are borne well above the silky or hairy leaves.

L. nánus—Small (4 to 16 inches), fragrant and annual, this blue-flowered species is native to grassy and brushy places in northeastern Nevada. Its flowers are in clearly separated groups and, according to some botanists, it has one or more subspecies in the California Coast Ranges and Sierra foothills.

L. stíveri—A clearly two-toned sort, 4 to 18 inches tall. The flowers have bright yellow standards and rose-pink or purple wings. It is at home in sandy or gravelly soils in the Sierras and southern Coastal Ranges. It is another annual.

L. subcarnósus—This is an annual and the official Bluebonnet and legally the State Flower of Texas. Growing up to 15 inches tall, it has long leaf stalks each bearing four to seven smooth segments. The smallish flowers in loose clusters are usually deep blue but sometimes white with a central greenish-yellow spot that turns red. At home in East and South Texas near the Gulf, it normally blooms in early spring.

L. texénsis—A little taller than the above and early summer-blooming, this is the one many people think of as the Texas bluebonnet, especially since it grows over most of Texas. It also differs in that not only both sides of its leaves are silvery-silky but also its leaf buds. To add to the confusion, the flowers are purple or lilac with a yellow or reddish blotch on the standards.

L. villósus—Often called the Lady Lupine, it has lilac or purplish flowers with a distinct red-purple spot on the standards giving it a two-toned look. Further, it is distinguished by being shaggy (villose) all over. It is also a distinctly southern plant, blooming in April and May in sandhills and woodlands of the Coastal Plain from North Carolina to Florida, Mississippi and Louisiana.

Culture: Except for transplanting, there are no difficulties in their culture. Just give them a poor, sandy, or gravelly soil, preferably acid, where drainage is good. They are short-lived in heavy soils and can't stand poorly-drained ones. The roots are strong and deep, making the moving of older established plants difficult. Therefore, if it is ever necessary to salvage plants from the path of construction concentrate upon the younger ones. Early fall is the best time, with early spring, as growth is commencing, next.

For the same reason, division of old plants is not too dependable a procedure in addition to the fact that the plant does not divide as fast as most perennials. Much more dependable—and the only method with the annual species—is the sowing of seeds. However, the seed coats are extremely hard and germination is slow and unreliable unless a small nick is cut through the seed coats and the seeds soaked overnight in water. Then sow in sandy soil in outside beds or in flats. When large enough to handle, move to regular or peat pots or to make setting out easier. Also, if no lupines have been present for many years, wet the seeds and roll them in Nod-o-gen or other inoculant for nitrogen-fixing bacteria before planting.

Wintergreen and Partridgeberry
Gaulthéria procúmbens and *Mitchélla répens*

Descriptions: Once again we shall discuss two different plants, not because they are very closely related—they are not—but because they are often confused in the public mind. Both are small, are groundcovers, evergreen, are found over somewhat the same range and both produce tasty berries relished by birds and small boys.

Where They Grow: See below.

Blooming Season: July and August in the case of the first and slightly earlier for the other.

G. procúmbens—Wintergreen or Checkerberry is generally found in evergreen or mixed woods where the soil is acid (about pH 5 or so) and in sun or part shade from Newfoundland and Manitoba south to Minnesota, Georgia and Alabama. More often than not, the soil is on the dry side.

It is a low, semi-woody plant producing erect perennial stems which rise to a height of 3 to 6 inches from creeping underground stems. The leaves are several, oval, 1 to 2 inches long, thickish, evergreen, shining dark green above and paler beneath. The flowers, which are white or pinkish, are bell-shaped, like those of the blueberry, and eventually give way to mealy round bright red berries ¼ to ½ inch in diameter. Very long-lasting, these fruits often hold well into the next season and retain their true wintergreen flavor to the end.

Culture: Because of its trailing nature, transplanting is not easy unless one is able to take up large sods such as are usually found on rock ledges. Only when an area is in danger from road construction is other moving advisable. A much safer method of propagation is to take cuttings of the new wood in early summer and root them in moist sand or sand and peat. Still better is to take the thinly rooted runners and treat them as cuttings. Results are much faster. Seeds, too, can be used, but the runner method is quickest.

/————/

M. répens—Partridgeberry, Twinberry. A lower plant which creeps openly over the surface of the soil. The leaves are evergreen, paired, much smaller than those of the above (¼ to ¾ inches long) and have conspicuous white veins. The flowers are white, waxy, fragrant, and borne in pairs united at the base. Because of this union, the berries are flattened, composed of two parts fused together, bright red and somewhat smaller than the round ones of the wintergreen. Like them, however, they are mealy, edible, and have a pleasant minty flavor.

A plant of the dryish woods, usually under pines or hemlocks, the partridgeberry is a native from Newfoundland to western Ontario and Minnesota, south to Florida and Texas. The need for shade, of course, increases as one goes farther south. Like the above, it prefers an acid soil and will last for many years. In the event of attack by slugs or snails, scatter a little of any good, approved bait between the plants.

Propagation: May be by seeds, stem cuttings, or runners as above, but this plant, being less woody, takes root much sooner and at almost any season. Also, because of more roots, transplanting is easier.

Wood Sorrel—*Óxalis montána*

Description: A very close relative of the European wood sorrel, *O. acetosélla*, and one of the daintiest of woodland plants. Its frail-looking flowers, borne singly on 3- to 5-inch stems, are 5-petaled, about 1 inch across, white or pinkish, striped with wine, and have a notch at the end.

The leaves are 3-parted, the individual segments heart-shaped and, like the flowers, rise directly from the creeping, scaly-toothed rootstocks which creep about just under the surface of the forest humus. Each night the leaves fold and open in the morning. The fruit is a tiny 5-celled capsule 1/6 of an inch long.

Where They Grow: Wood sorrels are natives of the cool, damp woods from Newfoundland to Saskatchewan and south in the mountains to North Carolina and Tennessee in deep, acid humus.

Blooming Season: This varies anywhere from May to July or even to mid-August according to geographical location, slope, and altitude.

Culture: This plant is one that requires shade and a cool, moist humus with pH 4 to 5. Here it revels with such companions as clintonia, creeping snowberry, dwarf mountain cranberries, and the bunchberries. Wherever you see these plants, wood sorrel will grow. For tree companions it chooses such ones as the northern spruces (white or black), balsam fir and, farther south, hemlocks. It is not the easiest plant to grow unless conditions are to its liking, but those being favorable, it spreads rapidly. It is a plant worth extending oneself to restore in desirable locations.

Transplanting is easy. All one needs to do is to take up large sods from any place where danger of construction threatens. This can be done at any season. Propagation by seed is possible but rarely, if ever, practiced. However, careful division of the rootstocks is readily accomplished.

Other Species: *O. oregána*—Another moist woods plant, its leaves whose blades are nearly 2 inches across, all spring from a rhizome. The pink or white flowers, on 2 to 6-inch stems, appear April to September. From Upper California's Coast Ranges to Washington's Olympics, east across the Cascades.

O. trillifólia—This one grows up to 8 inches tall and has leaf blades 2 to 3 inches across. The flowering branch has three to 15 white or pinkish blooms. It is found in meadows and moist woods from northwestern California to western Washington.

O. violácea—Violet Wood Sorrel. Another dainty woodland species. Its leaves are similar but it bears 3 to 6 rosy-purple flowers on each stem. Its range is from Maine to Minnesota, and Colorado, south to Florida and Texas, where it grows in somewhat drier, less acid (pH 6 to 6.5) woods.

Yellow Stargrass—*Hypóxis hirsúta*

Description: An interesting little plant which, like the blue-eyed grass, is a surprise package: just another grass until it blooms. Really they are small bulb-producing plants of the amaryllis family.

The small flowers, about ½ inch across, are 6-parted, bright yellow, starlike when open and come in clusters of 1 to 7 atop modest 6-inch stems. The leaves are of about the same height, about ¼ inch wide and all rise directly from a little round bulb ¼ to ½ inch in diameter. The fruit is a small, ball-like capsule containing several angled blank seeds.

Where They Grow: In open woods and grasslands in acid soil from Maine to Manitoba, south to Florida and Texas.

Blooming Season: Late April to July with occasional blooms in August and September.

Other Species: Some botanists have broken the stargrasses into a number of other species such as:

H. leptocárpa (Slender-fruited)—From the hammocks, woods, and bottomlands, Virginia to Missouri, south to Florida and Texas; *H. micrántha* (Tiny-flowered)—From the pinelands, bogs, and sandy clearings from Virginia to Florida and Texas; *H. séssilis* (Stemless-flowered)—A very local sort from the pinelands of Virginia south to Florida and Texas; *H. lóngi* (Long's)—An extremely local species from the damp, peaty and sandy open areas of Virginia. For our purposes, however, the differences are so small it is best to consider them all as one species and treat them the same.

Culture: While these stargrasses will grow in ordinary soils, almost without exception they seem to do better in acid, sandy ones generally in open woods. The basic species, for instance, is often found growing in open deciduous woods composed of various oaks, tuliptrees, dogwoods, etc., along with such smaller plants as false lily-of-the-valley, bayberries, azaleas, greenbrier, and assorted grasses. In fact, interspersing a fairly thick stand of false lily-of-the-valley, the yellow stargrass made one of the best combinations for such a location I have ever seen.

Given the proper soil and surroundings, it makes one of the easiest and most reliable of small plants. Set out 5 or 6 inches apart in groups of a dozen or more, placing the little bulblets only an inch deep, at the most. Sometimes it is recommended that it be combined with the blue-eyed grass (Sisyrinchium) but this advice is based more upon color harmonies than cultural preferences. The blue one likes moist places, the yellow, dry.

The stargrasses may be transplanted at any time of year, even in full bloom. Propagation is equally easy. They can be raised from seed sown in pots or in a protected place outside. They multiply moderately fast by themselves and can be divided.

INDEX

Aaron's rod, see Carolina thermopsis
Abronia alpina, 39
  fragrans, 40
  umbellata, 39
Acacia greggi, 40
Aconitum columbianum, 39
Actaea pachypoda (Actaea alba), 35, 42, 52
Actaea rubra, 35, 42, 52
Acer pensylvanicum, 35
Acorus calamus, 33, 34, 167
Adiantum pedatum, 35
adobe lily, 39
agave, misc., 40
Alnus incana, 33
alpine azalea, 36
  goldflower, 38
  heather, 39
  lily, 38
  mertensia, 15, 38
  shooting star, 39
Althaea,
  officinalis, 127
  rosea, 127
Amelanchier canadensis, 33, 35
American lily-of-the-valley, 36
American lotus *(Nelumbo lutea)*, 34, 166
American yew *(Taxus canadensis)*, 35
Amianthium muscaetoxicum, 37
Anaphilis margaritacea, 32
Anemone
  canadensis, 45
  cylindrica, 45
  deltoidea, 45
  multifida, 45
  nuttalliana, 46
  occidentalis, 38, 45
  parviflora, 46
  quinquefolia, 31, 34, 46
  virginiana, 46
Anemonella thalictroides, 31, 34, 46
Appalachian avens, 37
Aquilegia caerulea, 38, 64
  canadensis, 64
  chrysantha, 46
  elegantula, 46
  fomosa, 38, 46
  pubescens, 46
Arctostaphylos uva-ursi, 36, 53
Arenaria groenlandica, 36
Arethusa *(Arethusa bulbosa)*, 15, 34, 97, 105, 138
Argemone corymbosa, 40
Arisaema,
  dracontium, 33, 42, 119
  triphyllum, 33, 42, 119
aronia, 97, 137
arrow arum *(Peltandra virginica)*, 34

arrowhead *(Sagittaria latifolia)*, 14, 34, 41
arrow-leaved violet *(Viola sagittata)*, 162
Asarum arifolium, 169
  canadense, 33, 35, 42, 169
  candatum, 38, 169
  grandiflorum, 169
  hartwegi, 169
  lemmoni, 169
  shuttleworthi, 37, 169
  virginicum, 169
Asclepias
  amplexicaulis, 32, 59
  incarnata, 32, 59
  purpurascens, 32, 59
  quadrifolia, 32, 59
  syriaca, 13, 32, 40
  tuberosa, 13, 19, 25, 27, 28, 32, 37, 59
Asplenium platyneuron, 35
Aster, 24, 32, 35, 40, 42, 47, 48
  adscendens, 39
Aster
  alpigenus, 47
  chilensis, 39
  cordifolius, 47
  laevis, 47
  lateriflorus, 47
  linearifolius, 47
  modestus, 47
  novae-angliae, 47
  novi-belgi, 47
  pancicipitatus,, 47
  puniceus, 47
  spectabilis, 47
avalanche lily *(Erythronium montanum)*, 15, 38, 158

bake-apple berry *(Rubus chamaemorus)*, 15, 34, 146
baneberry *(Actaea)*, 14, 52
Baptisia leucophaea, 15, 37
barrel cactus, 39
barrel cactus, see ferocactus
barren strawberry, see waldsteinia
Bartonia aurea, 150
bayberry *(Myrica pensylvanica)*, 15, 32, 36
beach heath *(Hudsonia tomentosa)*, 36, 116
beach lupine *(Lupinus chamissonis)*, 170
beach pea, 14
beach plum, 15
bearberry *(Arctostaphylos uva-ursi)*, 15, 36, 53
beargrass, 39
bedstraw bellflower *(Campanula aparinoides)*, 57
bee-balm, 40
beech, 35
bellwort *(Uvularia perfoliata)*, 35

175

THE COMPLETE BOOK OF ROSES
Gerd Krüssmann
"A monumental and authoritative work . . . the definitive study of the rose from prehistoric times to 1981 . . ."
Gil Daniels, President, The American Horticultural Society.
"An indispensible and classic work in horticultural literature . . . recommended as a reference for all serious rosarians." Jarold Goldstein, Executive Director,
The American Rose Society

436 pages/300 illustrations	8½x11	hardbound

MEDIAEVAL GARDENS
John Harvey
An account of a neglected period in the history of the garden that reveals unexpected insights into the society of the time. Many strikingly beautiful illustrations taken from manuscripts, paintings, stained-glass windows, and other sources.
216 pages/11 color and 95 b&w photos 5 maps & plans 7x10 hardbound

JAPANESE MAPLES
J.D. Vertrees
"Finally, the first comprehensive work on Japanese maples . . . a wonderful job . . ." *Pacific Horticulture.*
"Authoritative . . .enjoyable reading . . . a beautiful and valuable book . . ."
American Horticulturist

192 pages/200 color plates	9x12	hardbound

TREES AND SHRUBS FOR WESTERN GARDENS
Gordon Courtright
" . . . pictorial companion to the *Sunset Western Garden Book* . . . a landmark effort and the only book in print to picture so many Western garden plants in color . . ." *Sunset Magazine.*

250 pages/800 color plates	9x12	hardbound

RHODODENDRON SPECIES, Volume I: Lepidotes
H.H. Davidian
For each species, a full botanic description as well as a discussion of the plant's discovery, introduction, cultivation, and cultural uses. In addition, a history of rhododendron expeditions, glossaries, and other supplementary tables and sections.

470 pages/97 color plates, 39 line drawings	8½x11	hardbound

THE TERRACE GARDENER'S HANDBOOK
Raising Plants on a Balcony, Terrace, Rooftop, Penthouse or Patio
Linda Yang
" . . . complete, carefully detailed, covering thoroughly and clearly every phase . . ."
National Council State Garden Clubs
" . . .tells how to make the most of cramped quarters . . ." *New York Times Book Review*

283 pages/112 photos,	32 line drawings	5½x8½	softbound

GARDENING IN THE SHADE
Harriet K. Morse
Nearly every garden has some shady spots which need special treatment; city gardeners receive limited sunlight because of surrounding buildings; and indoor gardeners are restricted to plants which grow in little or no light. This book is useful for almost every gardener in almost every situation.

242 pages/32 photos	5½x8½	softbound

Continued

WITHOUT A THORN: A Guide to Rose Gardening in the Pacific Northwest
Stu Mechlin & Ellen Bonanno
" . . .the 'must' rose handbook for the new regional gardener and an excellent review and reference book for the established rosarian . . ."   *The Oregonian*
100 pages/300 illustrations   5½x8½   softbound

PENJING The Chinese Art of Miniature Gardens
The first book to come out of China on this ancient horticultural art. The technique of miniaturizing plants and the creation of miniature gardens with water and mountain scenes is graphically demonstrated.
166 pages/80 color plates,   72 b&w photos   30 line drawings   8½x11
hardbound

THE ESSENTIALS OF BONSAI
One of the finest Bonsai books for the beginner to the intermediate enthusiast. It covers all the tools, plant material, and care as well as giving an excellent background.
108 pages/26 color photos, many b&w photos and line drawings 7½x8½
hardbound

HOW TO IDENTIFY FLOWERING PLANT FAMILIES A Practical Guide for Horticulturists and Plant Lovers
John Philip Baumgardt
Learn to analyze flower structure, construct a floral diagram, lay out a floral formula, and so fit a plant into its proper niche.
285 pages/57 color plates   122 illustrations   6x9   softbound

PLANT HUNTING IN NEPAL
Roy Lancaster
A group of horticultural botanists travelled through East Nepal collecting seeds of plants suitable for cultivation in Western gardens. As a result, many of these plants are now found in some of the most famous gardens in Europe.
194 pages/numerous color photos and line drawings   6x9   hardbound

POCKET GUIDE TO CHOOSING WOODY ORNAMENTALS
Gerd Krüssmann — translated by Michael E. Epp
A quick and easy reference for any design situation. A thesaurus of plant material for the professional, serious gardener.
141 pages   4½x7   flexible binding

ROCK GARDENING A Guide to Growing Alpines and Other Wildflowers in the American Garden
H. Lincoln Foster
This is a book of lasting value for the advanced rock gardener as well as the beginner, whether or not he has a green thumb.
466 pages/many line drawings   5½x8½   softbound

GETTING STARTED WITH RHODODENDRONS AND AZALEAS
J. Harold Clarke
The facts about rhododendrons and azaleas are all here, organized for handy reference in clear, concise, and lively language.
293 pages/73 b&w photos   5½x8½   softbound

PACIFIC NORTHWEST GUIDE TO HOME GARDENING
Ray N. McNielan and Micheline Ronningen
Some of the natural hardiness and competitiveness of plant life has been lost and today's hybrid food crop plants must be given special environmental care to flourish. This book gives you that information. It is basically a do-your-own-gardening book adapted to the Northwest.
298 pages/many illustrations and charts   6x9   softbound

TIMBER PRESS
P.O. Box 1631   Beaverton, Oregon 97075